Woodlands Trail
HANDBOOK

SECOND EDITION

Trail Life

Belton, South Carolina

Woodlands Trail Handbook
Published by Trail Life USA, Incorporated
dba Worthy Trailman Press
10612 Augusta Road
Belton, SC 29627 www.TrailLifeUSA.com

This book or parts thereof may not be reproduced in any form, stored in a retrieval system, or transmitted in any form by any means—electronic, mechanical, photocopy, recording, or otherwise—without prior written permission of the publisher, except as provided by United States of America copyright law.

Unless otherwise noted, all Scripture quotations are from the English Standard Version (ESV)

Copyright © 2017, 2019, 2021, 2023 by Trail Life USA, Incorporated. All rights reserved.

International Standard Book Number: ISBN# 978-1-7330259-3-5

While the author has made every effort to provide accurate telephone numbers and Internet addresses at the time of publication, neither the publisher nor the author assumes any responsibility for errors or for changes that occur after publication.

Second Edition, first printing

Printed in the United States of America.

ACKNOWLEDGMENTS

Proper credit for the structure and flow of the Woodlands Trail program goes to the many volunteers from Program Teams that worked with dedication to develop the Trail Life USA program.

National Program Manager: Seth Morrow
Project Editor: Mark Hancock, CEO
Book Design: Anna Jelstrom
Illustrations: Leigh Elizabeth
Cover Design: Greg Lane

THIS BOOK BELONGS TO

Woodlands Trail Trailman _____
and his parents.   NAME

A member of Troop # _____, a ministry of

_____
                        CHARTER ORGANIZATION

in _____
                              CITY, STATE

Friends of the
WOODLANDS TRAIL

BOOK ONE
SECOND EDITION

Trail Life

Belton, South Carolina

Friends of the Woodlands Trail

by

John Burkitt with Jessica R. Everson

Illustrations by Leigh Elizabeth

ACKNOWLEDGMENTS

National Program Manager: Seth Morrow
Project Editor: Mark Hancock, CEO
Author: John Burkitt
Story Editor: Jessica R. Everson
Illustrations: Leigh Elizabeth
Book Design: Anna Jelstrom
Cover designs: Greg Lane

Contents

CHAPTER 1
Bramble and the Well — 9

CHAPTER 2
Bramble Goes Fishing — 19

CHAPTER 3
The Long Rain — 27

CHAPTER 4
Mister Beaver's Trouble — 33

CHAPTER 5
Willow the Otter — 39

CHAPTER 6
Crossing the Creek — 45

CHAPTER 7
Half and Half — 53

CHAPTER 8
Lost! — 60

CHAPTER 9
The Patsy — 69

CHAPTER 10
Bramble's Burrow — 77

CHAPTER 11
Bramble and Fletch — 87

CHAPTER 12
The Angry Spot — 94

CHAPTER 13
The Long Walk — 101

Meet

Bramble   *Fletcher*   *and Tracker*

The Friends of the Woodlands Trail

CHAPTER 14
Tracker in Charge   107

CHAPTER 15
The Cookout   116

CHAPTER 16
A Sure Sign   125

CHAPTER 17
A Muddy Rescue   136

CHAPTER 18
Giving Thanks   142

CHAPTER 19
Fire in the Back Grove   149

CHAPTER 20
Little Lost Skunk   155

CHAPTER 21
Tracker's Sour Note   165

CHAPTER 22
Bramble's Bedtime   171

CHAPTER 23
Mister Ranger's Flag   179

CHAPTER 24
The First Snow   187

CHAPTER 25
A Christmas Story   199

SAY HELLO TO
The Woodlands Pals Team   209

*These stories are dedicated to the people
who gave me constructive feedback over the years.
Thanks to them, this book now rests in your hands.*

John Burkitt

CHAPTER I
Bramble and the Well

It was a fine spring day in the Woodlands. The sky was blue, the trees were green once again, and the flowers bloomed bright. A curious, young fox named Bramble decided to take a walk.

Like all young foxes, Bramble loved to explore new places and discover new things. And, like all young foxes, nearly every place and thing was new to him.

Once, at Beaver Pond, Bramble saw how a rock dropped into the water made rings that grew wide and wider. Another time, in the meadow, he found a shiny white ball with dimples all around. When Bramble brought it home, Father Fox told him it was called a "golf ball," and that it meant humans had been nearby. Father Fox warned Bramble about the dangers of coming too close to humans. Bramble knew he should listen. But, to him, each new discovery was more thrilling than the last.

As Bramble walked this day, he wondered what

new things he might find. Before long, his curiosity had taken him far off his normal path. Bramble knew it wasn't safe to wander where his parents wouldn't know to look for him. But just as he was about to turn back, he reached a clearing and saw the Park Cabin.

Bramble had heard stories from his friends about the cabin, but he had never seen it himself. Some of the stories were so strange and frightening, he wondered if they were really true. Like about fantastic sounds and voices that came from a box inside its tree-log walls. And its square eyes that glowed bright at night. And, most curious of all, about a human, called "Mister Ranger," who lived there.

> *Bramble had heard stories about the cabin, but he had never seen it himself.*

Bramble knew he should be careful around humans. He'd heard awful stories about them. How they started forest fires, left trash in the meadows, and loved to frighten small creatures out of their wits! He knew he should turn around and run home as fast as he could. But Bramble's curiosity pushed him forward.

Bramble crept slowly and quietly into the clearing. He felt his ears twist back, listening for sounds

coming from the cabin. But Bramble heard nothing. He felt his eyes narrow, looking for the cabin's glowing eyes. But Bramble saw none. And, most curious of all, Bramble saw no Mister Ranger. Maybe the cabin wasn't dangerous after all.

Bramble thought about the safety rules Father and Mother Fox had taught him. "If you don't know what something is, find

When Bramble saw the old stone tower standing near the cabin, he forgot everything he'd been taught.

someone who does, or leave it alone," Father Fox had said. But when Bramble saw the old stone tower standing near the cabin, he forgot everything he'd been taught.

When Bramble reached the tower, he saw that it was actually a wall that surrounded a tunnel running straight down, deep into the earth. Over the tunnel's mouth, a wooden bucket dangled from a rope wrapped around and around a metal wheel. Bramble was so curious about this new and interesting discovery, he ignored the funny feeling in his stomach. He took one more look around, sniffing the air for danger,

then scrambled up the rugged wall and leapt into the bucket to get a closer look.

No sooner had Bramble squeezed his tiny red body into that bucket, he felt himself plunge with a terrible suddenness, deep into the dark underground. Bramble squeezed his eyes shut and held his breath. Before he could cry for help, he heard a splash, and water—colder than he'd ever felt—showered his body from above. Bramble was no longer falling. But, when he opened his eyes, all he saw were the dark walls of the tunnel. The bucket and Bramble were sinking!

Bramble began to shiver. And, oh, did he cry! Harder than he had cried in his whole life! If only he hadn't let his curiosity guide his choices. If only he had listened to Father and Mother Fox's warnings about new and unknown things. Bramble felt quite sorry for himself.

But then, Bramble remembered something. He remembered another lesson Father and Mother Fox had taught him. They'd taught him that God is always there, and that He would always listen if he cried out to Him for help. PROVIDENCE 6a,b,c So, as the icy water poured over the top of the bucket, Bramble began to pray. He looked up to the little circle of blue sky and cried, "Help me! Please, God, help me!"

Bramble listened for an answer, but none came. By now, the bucket was under water, and the little fox was furiously kicking to stay afloat. He didn't know

Bramble felt himself plunge with a terrible suddenness...

how much longer he could keep swimming. He was afraid no one would ever find him.

"Help me!" he yipped again, as loud as he could. Again, there was no answer. If only he had told Mother and Father where he was going!

> *He was afraid no one would ever find him.*

But then, just at that moment, a face appeared over the edge of the stone wall. It was a man's face! Bramble didn't think things could get any worse. He watched the man grab the crank that held the rope above him. Then he begin to turn it, and the wooden bucket slowly came back under Bramble and carried him up the long tunnel and toward the light. But as Bramble came closer and closer to the top, he also came nearer to the man.

Bramble was terrified. He crouched low in the bucket, but also tried to look frightening, showing his teeth and growling. The man did not seem afraid.

"Hello there, little fellow," he said and pulled Bramble from the bucket.

"No! Please don't eat me!" Bramble cried.

The man laughed a deep rolling laugh, then held Bramble gently against his chest. Bramble ducked his head low. He was shivering cold. The man took off his jacket and wrapped it around the little fox, making him feel snug and warm.

"That well is dangerous," the man said and scratched Bramble behind his ears. "I should put a lid over it."

Bramble couldn't wait to tell his friends he'd not only seen the Park Cabin, he'd actually met Mister Ranger.

Bramble was still shaken from his experience, but he was feeling a bit more courageous. Even kind of safe. His tail wagged a bit, poking out beneath the man's jacket. Bramble looked up into the man's eyes. "Who are you?" he asked.

"You can call me Mister Ranger. I live here at the Park Cabin."

So this was Mister Ranger! Bramble couldn't wait to tell his friends he'd not only seen the Park Cabin, he'd actually met Mister Ranger. Now he had a story of his own!

"I'm Bramble," he said. "I live in the Woodlands with my Father and Mother. My sister and all my friends live there, too. Would you like to be my friend as well?"

Mister Ranger smiled. "I'd be delighted."

Bramble closed his eyes for one more ear scratch from his new friend.

Once he was dry, Bramble decided it was time to get home. He knew Father and Mother Fox would be worried by now. He said goodbye to Mister Ranger and ran off into the Woodlands.

> *Bramble closed his eyes for one more ear scratch from his new friend.*

As he made his way home, evening set in around him. The clouds turned golden, and the first few stars peeped out in the sky. Bramble thought about all the things he had seen on his walk. He thought about the things Mister Ranger taught him, too. About how the box of sounds and voices was called a "radio." And the cabin's glowing eyes were actually just "windows." Finally, Bramble reached the outside of his den.

"Is anyone home?" he called out.

Mother Fox shot out of the doorway, her eyes wide with fear. "Where have you been? Your Father and I have looked everywhere for you!" she cried, then threw her paws around Bramble, squeezing and kissing him. Bramble knew then how much his choices had caused his family pain. He felt very sorry.

Bramble rested his face against his mother. "I'm sorry, Mother. I'm sorry I scared you, and I'm sorry I didn't follow the rules. I know I shouldn't have wandered off." Bramble started to cry. "I promise I will never go where you can't find me again.

"It's okay, little one." his mother said. "I'm just so thankful you're back and that you're okay."

Once inside, Father and Mother Fox listened to Bramble's story. They couldn't believe how close he had come to being lost forever at the bottom of a well.

"Mister Ranger said he would be my friend." Bramble told them. "Is that all right?"

Mother Fox smiled. "He is a good friend to have. He once helped me when I was young, and now he's helped you, too."

"That's right," said Father Fox. "We all owe Mister Ranger a big thank you for rescuing you today."

"Yeah. But there's something I don't understand." Bramble said. "I asked God to help me, like you taught me. But He didn't answer back. Why didn't God get me out of the well?" PROVIDENCE 6a,b,c

Father Fox smiled. "God did help you, son. He made sure Mister Ranger was there to hear you."

"Oh!" Bramble said. "I guess you're right! Thank you, God."

"Yes." Father Fox said. "Now let's all bow our heads and thank God for hearing our prayers today."

And so the three foxes joined paws right there in their den and thanked God for always being there.

CHAPTER 2
Bramble Goes Fishing

It was a beautiful summer morning, but Bramble was not outside enjoying the sunshine. He was supposed to be at Silver Creek Pond with Father Fox learning how to fish. But Father Fox could not go.

Father Fox had a cold.

Bramble was disappointed. He had so looked forward his first fishing trip ever.

"It is a shame you two can't go fishing today," Mother Fox said. "It's so nice out, and we have not had trout for dinner in a long time."

"I know, dear. But as soon as I feel better, I'll—ah—ah—ACHOO!"

Mother Fox kissed Father Fox's cheek. "Now, now, dear. All you need to do right now is rest. There will be other days."

That's when Bramble got an idea. "Dad, may I borrow your fishing pole?"

"Borrow my fishing pole?" Father Fox said. "You know a fishing pole is not a toy." STEWARDSHIP 5a,b

"I know, Father. I just thought maybe I could catch a trout for dinner," Bramble said. "A big, juicy one we can all share."

"Bramble, fishing is a skill to be learned, just like digging a burrow or following tracks. You haven't had any—ah—ah—ACHOO!" Father Fox blew his nose noisily into a handkerchief. "You haven't had any practice, Bramble, and I don't want you to be disappointed if you don't catch a fish on your first try."

> "Bramble, fishing is a skill to be learned, just like digging a burrow or following tracks…"

"Maybe you should wait until your father can teach you," Mother Fox suggested. "He will surely feel well soon."

"But I'm sure I could catch a fish!" Bramble's face beamed at the thought of surprising everyone with his fishing skills. Surely it couldn't be that hard. Just last week, his friend, Tracker, caught three fish in one morning.

Father Fox looked at Mother Fox and smiled, then ruffled Bramble between the ears. "Okay. You may borrow it. But promise you won't get too upset if you don't catch anything. I'll be happy if you just do your best. And, please, be careful."

"Oh, I will! I will!" Bramble bounced with joy as he grabbed the fishing pole and tore out of the den with such speed, he almost didn't hear his mother calling after him.

"Bramble! Bramble, wait!" Mother Fox said. "Aren't you forgetting something?"

Bramble walked back inside the den. What could he be forgetting? Then he smiled, ran across the den, and kissed Mother Fox goodbye.

"That's nice, dear," Mother Fox said, "and I'll take your kisses anytime. But I meant you should thank your father."

"Oh! I forgot!" Bramble said. "Thanks, Dad!"

Bramble wasted no time on his way to Silver Creek Pond. Ordinarily, he would have become distracted as he followed the trail, curious about this new sound or that new sight. But all he could think of today was catching a big, juicy trout. He was sure he would catch

something, even if it was his first try. All he needed to do was put the hook in the water and wait for a fish to grab it, right?

Bramble reached the banks of Silver Creek Pond and found the place Father Fox once took him to chase frogs. To his surprise, his friend, Tracker, the young mountain lion, was sitting there with his fishing pole in hand.

Bramble was younger than Tracker, so he did not want Tracker to know this was his first time fishing. He couldn't wait to show Tracker that he, too, could catch a fish.

"Hi, Tracker!" Bramble said. "Do you mind if I fish with you? I'm going to catch a big, juicy trout for my family."

"Sure, Bramble." Tracker cleared the leaves off the smooth stone next to him and motioned for Bramble to sit. "The fish are sure biting today. I've caught two trout already!"

"Wow!" Bramble said, and sat next to Tracker. He tried to copy Tracker's moves without him noticing. He figured if he did everything Tracker did, he would catch a big, juicy trout, too!

Bramble saw how Tracker held his fishing pole, slinging the line into the water. Bramble did the same. He saw how Tracker twitched his wrist, causing the line to jump in the water a bit. Bramble twitched his wrist the same. Bramble felt very proud of himself. He was fishing!

Tracker watched Bramble closely and smiled. "You must be very good at fishing if you don't need bait."

"Bait?" Bramble asked, then laughed nervously. "Oh, sure. How could I forget." But Bramble did not know what "bait" was or what to do with it.

"First time fishing, huh, Bramble?"

Bramble was embarrassed by the truth. He looked down at the ground and kicked at the pebbly sand. "Well . . ."

"You know, Bramble, everyone needs help learning to do new things. You should never be afraid to ask someone to teach you."

Bramble looked up at Tracker. He didn't look like he

"First time fishing, huh, Bramble?"

was making fun of him, and it made Bramble relax.

"I guess I just didn't want to look dumb."

"Asking questions is never dumb, Bramble. And once you know how to fish properly, I'm sure you'll be great!" Tracker leaned forward and picked a single worm from the twisty, squirmy pile in front of him and held it up in the air.

"... everyone needs help learning to do new things. You should never be afraid to ask someone to teach you."

"Eww!" Bramble said. "What's that for?"

"We use worms to help us catch fish. Worms may not sound good to you, but fish love worms."

"Oh," Bramble said. "I get it. The worms are bait!"

"That's right, Bramble."

"Can I use some of your worms—I mean, *bait?*" Bramble asked.

"How about I show you how to dig up worms, and then you'll always know where to get bait when you need it." Tracker led Bramble to a patch of soft dirt by the bank and began to scratch around. Before long

he had plenty of worms for bait. Bramble dug next to Tracker until he got a few worms of his own. He poked one with his paw. "Eww!" Bramble wrinkled his nose. "They're all wet and wiggly!"

Tracker laughed. "If you were a fish, you'd think they were juicy and yummy."

Bramble laughed and wiped his paw in the grass. "No thanks! I think I'd rather be a fox."

"Yeah," Tracker said. "I think you're right." They both laughed together. Bramble was learning so much.

Next, Tracker showed Bramble how to hold a worm securely without squishing it, and Bramble baited his hook on the very first try.

CHAPTER 3

The Long Rain

It was springtime in the Woodlands, but you couldn't tell to look outside. The sun was playing hide and seek, and the sky was covered in a curtain of clouds, gray and gloomy. As if that wasn't bad enough, it was raining. In fact, it had been raining for days. Not just little showers, but the kind of heavy rain that keeps all the leaves dancing and all the mud puddling.

No one was going out in this weather.

Tracker the mountain lion sat near the door of his family's cave. His mother, father, and his sister, Violet, were nearby, each keeping busy with this or that. But not Tracker. Tracker wasn't doing anything.

Tracker was bored.

"It's been raining for days. Is it ever going to stop?" Tracker asked his mother.

No one was going out in this weather.

"Of course it will," Mother Lion said, looking up from the blanket she was knitting.

"When?" Tracker asked.

"When it's ready to," she answered. "Maybe today, maybe tomorrow. Maybe even the day after that. In the meantime, just be glad you have somewhere to go and get out of the rain."

"But it's hard to be glad when I'm so bored," Tracker complained, his lip pouting. "And do you know why I'm so bored?"

> *"... it's hard to be glad when I'm so bored."*

"Because it's raining?" she asked.

"Yeah," Tracker sighed. "Boring ole rain!" Tracker's ears slumped low.

Father Lion had been making repairs around the cave, but after listening to Tracker's complaints, he stopped working to see if he could help. "Part of the problem is your attitude, son. Sure the rain can make things seem boring, but there are lots of things you can do when you can't play outside."

"I can't think of a thing," Tracker said. "Not one single thing."

Father Lion set down his tool bag and walked over to where Tracker sat. "It's been raining a very long time, and that's a fact. Still, when you're going through something bad, God always gives you a way out. Sometimes you just have to look for it." PROVIDENCE a,b,c

"How will I know when I've found it?" Tracker asked.

"It's hard to be glad when I'm so bored!"

"You'll know because you will feel better."

Tracker thought about that for a while then said, "Would you tell me a story, Dad?"

"Sure, son," Father Lion said. "Did I ever tell you about the time I tried to jump across Silver Creek?"

"Is this the one where you landed in the fishing hole, and the snapping turtle got after you?"

"Yes." Father Lion cleared his throat. "I suppose I've told you that one, huh?"

"Yeah," Tracker said. "Many times."

> *"It's bad enough being bored! A bath would make it unbearable!"*

"Okay," his father continued. "What about the time I tried to visit Mister Beaver, and—"

"And you got stuck in his front door, and it took you a whole hour to get out." Tracker shook his head. "You've told me that one, too, Dad."

Father Lion chuckled. "Well, so I did."

Mother Lion reached for another ball of yarn and said, "You know, Tracker, you could always take a bath."

"Nooooo!" Tracker begged. "It's bad enough being

bored! A bath would make it unbearable!"

Mother Lion laughed. "You know, when I was your age, I used to ask the clouds to stop raining."

Tracker frowned. "I've tried that. It doesn't work."

"Maybe if you ask them to keep on raining, that won't work either!"

"Very funny," Tracker said grumpily. "Besides, I tried that, too."

Just then, a dark shadow appeared at the cave door. But who could possibly be out in this weather?

"Hello," the shadow said, as it moved into the dim light of the cave.

"Oh!" Tracker laughed. "It's you, Bramble Fox! You're all wet!"

Bramble squeezed his eyes shut and shook from his head down to his tail, sending rain drops all over the cave. And all over Tracker. Any other time this might have made Tracker mad, but this time he was just happy to see his friend.

"Bramble! What brought you out in all this rain?" Mother Lion asked.

"I'm so bored! Bored, bored, bored! Boring ole rain,"

Bramble said.

Mother Lion laughed. "You sure do sound like someone else I know!"

"Really? Who's that?" Bramble asked.

Tracker grinned. "I think I know."

"Oh." Bramble laughed. "I think I know, too. But my father told me being with friends can make even the worst things seem not so bad."

> "... being with friends can make even the worst things seem not so bad."

"I sure hope so." Tracker said. "Either way, I'm sure glad you're here."

"Me too, Tracker. Me too."

A wonderful thing happened to Tracker and Bramble that day. They were still stuck inside, but, together, they thought of lots of fun things to do.

Tracker and Bramble were no longer bored.

So Father Lion was right. When you're going through something bad, God always gives you a way out. Sometimes you just have to look for it.

Or wait for it to show up at your door.

CHAPTER 4
Mister Beaver's Trouble

Bramble and Tracker walked down to Beaver Pond one morning. They found Mister Beaver there, working hard with sticks and mud, making repairs to his dam.

"Hello there!" Bramble said.

Mr. Beaver sighed deeply. "Hello boys. Nice day for an outing."

> *No one else in the Woodlands worked as hard as Mister Beaver.*

But Mister Beaver did not sound like he thought it was a nice day. In fact, he looked quite sad.

No one else in the Woodlands worked as hard as Mister Beaver. As the waters of Silver Creek made their way to the far-off sea, Mister Beaver built dams to hold some of it back so that his Woodlands friends could have a pond all year long.

But water doesn't always cooperate. When some-

thing stands in its way, it will find cracks and holes to push through. And if those small leaks aren't stopped, they will quickly grow into big ones.

That's what was happening to Mister Beaver's dam. And that's why Mister Beaver was working so hard.

"Just look at all the trash in this pond!" Mister Beaver waved his hand out over the clutter of empty cans, bottles, and trash that littered the water and banks. "All this showed up after last night's big rain. Trash from the campers at the picnic grounds. But there's no time to clean it now. I must fix this dam, or we'll soon have no pond."

> *"Just look at all the trash in this pond!"*

"It does look terrible," Tracker said.

"It's not just how bad it looks. It's disrespectful. Not just to you and me, but to God's beautiful creation! I suppose I'll have to get to it when I can." With that, Mister Beaver returned to his work, grumbling to himself as he went. "I don't get to eat their food, oh no! But I sure get stuck cleaning up their mess!"

Tracker sighed. The corners of his mouth dropped

as he watched Mr. Beaver. "I heard that last summer a duck got caught in someone's old fishing line. If Mister Beaver hadn't helped him, he would have drowned."

Bramble shook his head. "If Mister Ranger catches those campers throwing their trash on the ground, he'll make them leave for sure. This is why we have rules!"

"Yeah, but Mister Ranger can't be everywhere or see everything." Tracker said. "He has to rely on his helpers."

"Like us?" Bramble asked.

> *"Mister Beaver is always helping others. It's time someone helps him."*

"Exactly." Tracker said.

Bramble thought about that. "You know, Mister Beaver is always helping others. It's time someone helps him."

Tracker smiled. "You're absolutely right, Bramble. Let's do it! Let's help Mister Beaver clean up all this trash."

"I'm with you, Tracker," Bramble said. "Let's get to work!"

And so they did. Tracker and Bramble pitched in

right away. It felt good helping Mister Beaver. They even made a game out of it to see who could make the biggest pile of trash. Before long, the pond was shaping up, and they had made two huge piles. Even better, Mister Beaver was smiling again.

"You don't know how much this means to me, boys," he told them. "It's nice to see someone else cares about this forest as much as I do."

By lunchtime, they had almost finished.

"Wait a minute," Tracker said. "We've been working so hard to gather the trash, we didn't think about what we would do with it!"

"You're right, Tracker. I've been so busy trying to make my pile the biggest, I never thought about it," Bramble said. "So what now?"

"Someone will have to take it all to the dump," Tracker said. "But this is an awful lot of trash for us to move alone. Still, we'll have to come up with a plan before the next rain comes and washes it all back into the pond."

This news came as quite an upset for Tracker and Bramble. They were disappointed that they hadn't thought of it until now. What were they going to do?

Just when the boys were about to give up hope, Old

"It's nice to see someone else cares about this forest as much as I do."

MISTER BEAVER'S TROUBLE 37

Moe, the biggest bear in the forest, came out of the trees and walked over to where they sat.

"Looks like you boys have been hard at work," the old bear said. "But you have quite a lot left to do to get all this trash where it belongs. Why don't you two little fellas move back and let Old Moe handle this."

They were both a bit surprised. Old Moe was known for being kind of a grouch. But they weren't going to question him. It seemed like he really wanted to help.

"Are you going to take it all to the dump?" Bramble asked.

Old Moe smiled. "Sure am. We all need to do our part to make our community a nice place to live. Even an old bear like me has a role to play."

At the end of the day, Mister Beaver thanked Tracker and Bramble. "You are the best helpers I've ever had!" he said. "I may have built the pond, but you boys made it beautiful again. And you learned that a little hard work goes a long way."

"You're welcome, Mister Beaver," Tracker said. "It just goes to show, we can't expect someone else to make our world a better place. STEWARDSHIP 5a,b

We all have to chip in and work for it."

CHAPTER 5
Willow the Otter

Tracker and Bramble were fishing at Beaver Pond. Things were a bit slow, so Tracker decided to tell one of his funny stories.

"Once my sister Violet and I were crossing the stream at the ford . . ."

Bramble laughed. "I can already tell this is gonna' be a good one," he said. "Nobody tells a story like you, Tracker."

"Anything to keep my fans happy," the mountain lion teased, smiling proudly. "Anyhow, we were crossing the creek and the water was chilly, so Violet was walking across on stepping stones because she didn't want to get wet. Only one of the stones wasn't really a stone at all. It was this old turtle out sunning himself on the rocks. Well when Violet stepped on it, that turtle started—"

"Wait!" Bramble cut Tracker off mid-sentence.

"What?" Tracker asked, confused.

Bramble's ears twitched. "I hear a strange noise," he said.

"What kind of strange noise?" Tracker asked.

"Like rustling." Bramble said, then pressed a finger to his mouth. "Shhhh."

Kssh kssh kssh.

"There it goes again!"

> *Bramble's ears twitched. "I hear a strange noise," he said.*

"I heard it, too," Tracker said. "What do you think it is?"

I don't know. Maybe it's—"

"BOO!" shouted an otter cub as he charged from the tree line.

Bramble and Tracker both screamed, "AAAAAAAH!" and leapt in the water.

The otter stood on the shore and laughed, holding his sides. It was Willow, and he was laughing so hard, tears rolled down his cheeks.

Tracker and Bramble dragged themselves from the water and stomped onto the shoreline, grumbling the whole time.

"What a hoot!" Willow said to the boys. "Some fun, huh?"

"Some fun, huh?"

"Maybe for you," Bramble said, shaking himself off. "But it wasn't funny to us."

"Don't be so upset," Willow said. "It was just a little joke."

"The story Tracker was telling before you scared us half to death was 'just a little joke,'" Bramble said. "You made me drop my father's fishing pole in the water!" Bramble went back and fished around for it in the muddied water.

> *"Don't be so upset," Willow said. "It was just a little joke."*

"A joke is only funny when everyone can laugh," Tracker told Willow, as he scrambled to gather the worms he'd spilled.

"Well I thought it was funny," the otter said.

"It won't be so funny next time," Bramble warned.

"Aww c'mon, guys. Lighten up." Willow said. "Hey! Wanna' race?" he asked them. "I bet I could beat you to the other side of the pond and back."

"I know you can," Bramble said. "If you really want to race, why don't we race to the big oak tree and back?"

"That's not fair! You know I can't run fast with these short legs."

Bramble nodded. "Exactly. And you know I can't swim fast with these long legs. So let's do something fair for everyone. We'll see who can catch the biggest fish—and I mean with a fishing pole."

"Yeah, that sounds fun," Tracker said. "But if Willow wants to fish with us, he'll have to behave."

Willow looked surprised. "You mean you'll really let me fish with you? Even after I made you mad?"

"Of course." Tracker said.

"I've never fished with a pole before. But it might be fun to try. Is that okay with you, too, Bramble?"

"It will be if I ever find Father Fox's fishing pole," he said.

"A joke is only funny when everyone can laugh."

"I'm sorry, Bramble. And I'm sorry I scared you guys," Willow said. "I'll tell you what. I'm going to help you find that pole. And I'm going to help Tracker dig up some more worms. Then maybe he'll tell us the rest of the story." TRUTH 1c HUMAN DIGNITY 3b

WILLOW THE OTTER 43

"Why not?" Tracker said. "It's a real hoot!"

Bramble smiled. "I sure like being helped a whole lot better than I like being scared."

Willow nodded his head. "I get it. And I'm really sorry. It's definitely more fun hanging out with good friends than it is making them mad. I'll be sure to remember that next time."

"Yes, next time," Bramble said, then the three friends waded into Beaver Pond to find Father Fox's lost pole.

CHAPTER 6
Crossing the Creek

When Tracker and his sister Violet were young cubs, their mom and dad used to carry them on their backs if they needed to get across the creek. Then one day Dad told them they were getting too big to be carried.

"But you're strong enough, Dad," Tracker said. "I know you can do it."

"Oh, sure, I'm strong enough. But that's not the point," his father said. "You're big enough to learn how to swim now, and your mom and I will teach you."

Violet took Dad up on the challenge right away. Before long she could

Tracker panicked and had to be rescued.

bob across the creek like a stick. But when Tracker tried, his head dipped under the water, and he sucked a bunch of it up his nose. The water burned and made him gasp for air. He flailed his arms and kicked around, but couldn't find the ground to stand. Tracker panicked

and had to be rescued.

That experience scared Tracker so badly, he refused to try again. Nothing his mom or dad said could convince him to get back into the water. As much as they wanted to help him overcome his fear, they knew he would have to do it on his own.

After that day, when family outings took them across the creek, Tracker would have to run all by himself, way up the creek, to a spot where the stepping stones went from one side to the other. There, he could hop across the water.

Nothing his mom or dad said could convince him to get back into the water.

This always put Tracker far behind his family. It would take him so long to catch up that he often missed out on all the fun. Still, as much as he hated getting left behind, Tracker was too afraid to try swimming again.

Things went on that way for nearly a year until one cloudy and rather dull day Tracker found himself bored with nothing to do. He decided to visit his friend, Willow the Otter. So he rushed through the woods to Silver

Creek. When he got there, he found Willow building a fort . . . on the other side of the creek.

There was no way Tracker was going to swim across, but he really wanted to help with the fort. Building with Willow would surely cure his boredom. So he ran up the creek until he reached the stepping stones and joined Willow in working on the fort.

Tracker and Willow passed much of the day building and laughing and playing together but, after a while, the gray sky turned darker and the clouds spread out as far as you could see.

Then, it rained.

The rain did not bother Willow at all; otters love the water. In fact, they spend as much time wet as they do dry. But, like most cats, mountain lions hate to get wet.

Tracker looked up at the sky and frowned. It was coming down hard and fast. "Well, that's my cue to leave."

"Okay," Willow said. "I'll walk you to the other side of the creek."

The two walked together back to the place Tracker had crossed, but when they reached the spot, it looked

different. Where were the stepping stones?

"What's the matter, Tracker?" Willow asked.

"I can't find the stepping stones," he said. "They must be farther up the creek."

"No, they're right there," Willow explained, pointing toward the water. "See. The rain made the creek rise. The stones are just covered with water now. You'll have to swim across."

> How would he get home and out of the rain if he couldn't get across the creek?

Tracker was devastated. How would he get home and out of the rain if he couldn't get across the creek? Worse than that, he was worried that Willow would find out he couldn't swim and might tell all their friends! What about his reputation as a fearless mountain lion?

"I-I-I don't feel like swimming," Tracker stammered. "Maybe I'll just wait for the water to go back down."

"You might have a very long wait. Look at those clouds," Willow said, leaning back to look all around. "They're surrounding us on all sides."

"I can't wait that long." Tracker said. "Mom and Dad

will be looking for me."

Willow jumped into the creek and swam out a ways, searching for the stepping stones under the water.

"Isn't there another way across," asked Tracker.

Willow shook his head. "Nope. This is it."

Tracker plopped down on his hindquarters. "No thanks," he said. He hung his head low and thought about how scared he had felt the last time he went into the creek. How he'd tried so hard to hold his nose up, but the water still got in. And how badly it stung. Oh, he'd felt so helpless!

> *Tracker was helpless and soggy and embarrassed all at the same time. This was not going to work.*

But he also felt helpless being stuck on the wrong side of the creek, getting soggier by the minute. And he felt embarrassed that he was afraid to learn how to swim. He was helpless and soggy and embarrassed all at the same time. This was not going to work.

Suddenly, Tracker heard a familiar voice calling his name in the distance.

CROSSING THE CREEK

*The farther he went, the better he did.
Swimming wasn't so bad after all!*

"Tracker! Tracker!" It was his father, who soon came around the bush on the opposite side of the creek.

Tracker felt relieved at the sight of his father but still scared at the thought of crossing the creek.

His father jumped into the creek with Willow and swam out about halfway across.

"Looks like this is the best place to cross, Tracker," he said. "Jump in right here by me, and we will cross over together."

That's when he realized if he was ever going to get past his fear, now was the time.

That's when Tracker realized if he was ever going to get past his fear, now was the time. He stood up tall. His ears pointed forward, and his eyes narrowed in determination. He called out to Willow and his father. "I'll do it! I'll do it right now!"

And that's what he did.

He ran as fast as he could to the edge of the creek and leapt to his father, where the water was deep over his head. There was no turning back now. It was sink or swim.

Father and Willow came alongside him. "Paddle with all four paws," he called. "Just keep them moving! You can do it, Tracker!"

Tracker paddled hard and fast. He swallowed a little water and had to sneeze a few times when it got in his nose, but he managed to keep his head up. He was doing it! He was moving across the creek! And the farther he went, the better he did. Swimming wasn't so bad after all!

Once Tracker made it to the other side, he could swim as well as Violet. He was so proud of himself. He had conquered his fear!

Tracker shook the water from his coat, quickly gave a proud glance to his father, and waved bye to his friend. Then he and his father turned and ran all the way home.

As they ran his father said, "Tracker, you were brave today! I'm very proud of you."

And from that day forward, when Tracker went on family outings, he swam across the creek with his family.

And he never again missed out on any of the fun.

CHAPTER 7
Half and Half

Everyone knows that young mountain lions are always hungry. But this day, Tracker was especially hungry. He'd already eaten all the food his mother packed for him, but he was still far from home and could think of nothing but his grumbling belly.

"I'm still so far from home, and I'm starving!" he said.

Just then, Tracker spotted Willow the Otter under the shade tree near the bank. He was sitting with some freshly caught fish and a picnic basket. Tracker felt he had never seen anything more wonderful. His mouth watered on the spot. "Oh my! I wonder what his mother packed him today."

Tracker decided to go find out.

"Hello, Tracker!" Willow said when he saw his friend. "Got time for a visit?"

"Sure!" he said. "You read my mind." Tracker took a seat near the picnic basket. "Mind if I look to see

what's inside?"

"Sure. Go right ahead," he said.

Tracker opened the lid. The aromas inside the basket were so tempting, his stomach began to growl immediately. "Wow. Nice lunch, Willow." Tracker closed the lid, but his stomach kept growling. Then he got an idea. "Hey, Willow. I have an idea. If you share with me today, I'll share with you later. What do you think?"

TRUTH Ic

"Of course we can share, Tracker."

And so they did.

The aromas inside the basket were so tempting, his stomach began to growl immediately.

A week passed, and Tracker had almost forgotten about his promise to Willow. He was coming back from Silver Creek one day, carrying a bucket of fish he'd caught. "Hey there, fish!" he said, looking down into the bucket. "Mom and Dad are going to be so glad to see you. I'm inviting you all to join us for dinner, and I'm not taking no for an answer." Tracker laughed at his joke.

Just then Willow stepped from behind some nearby

54 FRIENDS OF THE WOODLANDS TRAIL

bushes. He was carrying a bucket too, but his was empty. "Hi, Tracker. Caught you some fish today?"

When Tracker saw it was his friend Willow, he decided to play a joke on him. He grinned mischievously. "Sure did. And one of them is no ordinary fish. Look." Tracker tilted the bucket toward Willow. "See that big one there?" he asked, pointing at the largest fish. "Ask him what he's up to, and he'll say, 'Nothing at all!'"

Willow scratched his head. "Really?" He leaned over the bucket and gave it a try. "Hello, Mister Fish. What are you up to?" The otter waited, but the fish didn't respond.

Tracker was right—the fish said nothing at all!

Eventually, Willow realized Tracker was pulling his leg. "Ha ha. Good one, Tracker. I'll have to try that on my father." Willow shook his head. "But, tell me Tracker, how did you do so well today? The fish weren't biting for me at all." He held his empty bucket out for his friend to see.

The mountain lion grinned. "That's because I have a secret fishing hole. Quite frankly, it's the best spot in all the Woodlands. There's a fish there so big, if I told you

about it, the story would weigh eight pounds!"

The otter chuckled. "You and your jokes, Tracker!" he said, but looked at the fish in Tracker's bucket

He held his empty bucket out for his friend to see.

again. "Seriously though. Do you really have a secret spot? Come on. Tell your old friend Willow the secret. I won't spread it around. Honest!"

Tracker remembered that Willow had shared his lunch when he was hungry and about the promise he'd made. If you share with me today, I'll share with you later. But sharing your lunch was one thing; giving away your best secret was quite another! The mountain lion thought a moment about what he should do.

Tracker remembered that Willow had shared his lunch when he was hungry and about the promise he'd made.

"Well, you did give me half of your lunch," Tracker said. "And I did promise I would share with you later. So, if I tell you, we'll be even, right?"

"Right!" Willow said, cheerfully.

"Okay," Tracker said, "here's what you do. Go to the bend in the creek where the big tree fell across. From there you can see a tall oak."

"Is that your fishing spot? By the oak tree?"

"No," Tracker said, "but it's halfway there."

"Okay, so I'm by the oak tree," Willow said. "What's next?"

Tracker grinned. "You shared half of your lunch with me, and I shared half my secret, so we're even."

Willow stood in shock. He didn't know what to say. He knew Tracker liked to joke, but this was just plain mean. "But that half of a lunch did you a lot of good, Tracker," he said. "After you ate, you weren't hungry anymore. What good will half your secret do me?"

Tracker laughed. "Ha ha! If only you had given me all your lunch, I would have told you all my secret. You can't be mad at me, Willow. Fair is fair."

Willow was very disappointed. "I thought you were my friend, Tracker. I'll remember this!" he said, then turned to leave.

Tracker threw his head back and laughed. "Oh, Willow. I'm just teasing you, buddy. Come back here."

Willow stopped and looked at Tracker. Tracker walked over to Willow and threw his arm over the otter's shoulders. "Of course I'll tell you the whole secret. You're my friend."

Willow felt relieved. For a second there, he'd really fallen for his friend's trick. "You got me again, Tracker."

"Oh, Willow. You should know me better than that. I would have shown you my secret spot even if you hadn't shared your lunch with me." TRUTH Ic

"And, I would have given you half my lunch even if you hadn't promised to share with me."

Tracker smiled, then bent to whisper the rest of the secret into his friend's ear.

From that day forward, Tracker and Willow knew the best secret of all, and it wasn't where to catch the biggest or the best fish. It was that nothing is more valuable than true friendship.

CHAPTER 8
Lost!

Everyone knew that Bramble could outrun Tracker, and Tracker could outjump Bramble. They had proven this time and time again. Still, they were always trying to beat each other. That's why one day, after Bramble won yet another race, Tracker said, "How about best two out of three?"

> *Tracker looked up, and there it was. The most beautiful butterfly he'd ever seen.*

Bramble laughed. "Face it, Tracker. You're never gonna' beat me," he said. "Everyone knows I'm . . ." Bramble's voice trailed off. He seemed distracted by something in the sky. "Hey, look at that butterfly! Have you ever seen one like that before?"

Tracker looked up, and there it was. The most beautiful butterfly he'd ever seen. Its wings were a shimmering blue and seemed to glow in the light of the

After a while their shiny blue rival seemed to tire of the game and perched itself on a tree branch.

sun. "Let's catch it!" he said. Without another word, they ran off in hot pursuit.

Now there are two things everyone should know about butterflies. First, butterflies can fly up and down as well as they fly back and forth. And second, they don't like to be caught. Needless to say, this butterfly led the two friends on a merry chase. After a while their shiny blue rival seemed to tire of the game and perched itself on a tree branch. There it could look down at the fox and mountain lion and flash its wings in triumph.

Unwilling to give up just yet, Tracker made a jump for it.

He came nowhere near the branch.

"I'll get it!" Bramble said and leapt as high as he could. But the fox, too, fell short of his target.

"Come on, Bramble. If I can't jump that high, what makes you think you can?" Tracker said. He shook his head. "Oh well. I guess he won this one. We might as well head back."

"Yeah," Bramble said. "It's too bad. I really wanted to get a look at him up close. Maybe next time."

Bramble looked around a bit, then said, "Uh,

Tracker? Where are we?"

Tracker looked left, and then he looked right. "Umm . . . I have no idea," he replied. "I thought you knew."

"I thought you knew!" said Bramble.

"Let's just head back the way we came," Tracker said. "I'm sure we'll recognize something soon." But as the friends walked along, they realized how different things looked from this new angle.

And there was something else.

"Tracker? Where are our tracks?" Bramble asked.

> *As the friends walked along, they realized how different things looked from this new angle.*

"The ground here is covered in pine needles. Pine needles don't show tracks."

Bramble's lip trembled. "What are we going to do?" he asked. "I don't like it here. I want to go home!"

"I know. So do I." Tracker said.

Now Bramble's whole body trembled. "T-T-Tracker, are we lost?"

Tracker sighed deeply. As much as he didn't want

to admit it, he was beginning to think they were. He didn't even know which direction was home. "I think so, Bramble."

"Oh no!" Bramble cried. "What if we can't get home? What if we never get home? Stupid old butterfly! I hate butterflies!"

Tracker gave Bramble's shoulder a pat. "You don't hate butterflies, Bramble, and you don't need to be afraid. We may be lost now, but our parents will come looking for us. I bet Mister Ranger will help, too. But there's something we can do to help them find us."

He didn't even know which direction was home.

"There is?" Bramble asked, sniffing back tears.

"Yes. We can stay here and let them come to us. Whenever you're lost, you should always stay in one place until you're found."

"And that works?" Bramble asked.

"Sure it does. Now let's pick some raspberries to eat. They'll make us feel better."

Tracker was right. Picking raspberries did make them feel better. They were lost, but at least they

weren't hungry and lost. And they were distracted from their troubles for a while. But they were still a little scared.

"I wish there was something else we could do to feel better," Bramble said.

Tracker smiled. "There is."

"What?" Bramble asked.

Tracker put his paws together. "Let's ask the Lord to give us courage," he said, then bowed his head.

Tracker and Bramble prayed together. They asked God to help those searching for them. And they asked for courage while they waited. Then they settled down under a shade tree to wait. PROVIDENCE 6a,b,c

Several hours passed. The sky turned soft and pink, and the stars winked in one by one. Just when Tracker began to think they'd have to spend the night under the tree, he heard footsteps over the dried pine needles.

The sky turned soft and pink, and the stars winked in one by one.

Crunch, crunch, crunch.

LOST! 65

"We're over here!" he called, hoping it was someone who'd come to rescue them.

A beam of light flickered through the trees. The footsteps came closer until . . .

"There you are, you little rascals. Are you two okay?"

It was Mister Ranger!

He put his arm around his friend and smiled proudly at Mister Ranger.

"Mister Ranger!" Tracker and Bramble cried in unison.

"You have no idea how worried your folks are," Mister Ranger told them. "The thought of you being out here all alone . . ."

"We were lost, but we weren't alone," Bramble told him. "Tracker and I had each other." He put his arm around his friend and smiled proudly at Mister Ranger.

"We had God, too," Tracker said.

"Yeah," Bramble agreed. "God, too."

"We prayed together, and then we stayed in one place so you could find us," Tracker explained.

Mister Ranger nodded. "I see you boys have been taught the best way to be found. When you stay in one place, you help those who are trying to find you," he explained. "And you know something else?"

"What," asked Tracker.

"God helped, too," he said.

"He did?" Bramble asked.

"Absolutely, Bramble. He helped by giving you wise parents to teach you how to be safe and how to be found. And, more importantly, to turn to Him whenever you are lost."

"That's true," Bramble said. "And he helped you find us, right, Mister Ranger?"

"Well, yes, that's true. It was God who helped guide my steps so I could find you."

"When you stay in one place, you help those who are trying to find you."

"I guess that kind of makes you the answer to our prayers," Tracker said.

Mister Ranger winked at him. "I guess you're right, Tracker. Now let's get back to your parents. And while we walk, we can thank God for keeping you safe today."

"And for giving us wise parents," Tracker added.

"And for guiding Mister Ranger to us," Bramble said.

So that's just what they did. As they walked by the light of Mister Ranger's flashlight, they thanked God for all those things and more.

CHAPTER 9
The Patsy

One day, while out practicing his hunting skills, Bramble saw a young otter not far from Silver Creek. From behind, it looked like his friend Willow, so he called out to him.

"Hey, Willow!" he said.

The otter turned to face Bramble. But it wasn't Willow. "My name's not Willow," the otter said. "I'm Tipper."

"Oh! Hi, Tipper. I'm Bramblewood, but you can call me Bramble. Whatcha' doing?"

"I'm dry fishing."

"What is dry fishing?"

"It's like regular fishing, but it's faster. And you don't need a fishing pole or bait. All you need is a patsy."

"Oh, I see," Bramble said, but he was still confused. "Uh, Tipper?" he said.

"What is it, Bramble?"

"What's a patsy?" he asked.

"Heh heh. You don't know what a patsy is? And I thought foxes were supposed to be clever."

The way Tipper looked at Bramble embarrassed him. It gave him a funny feeling inside, like maybe this wasn't the kind of friend he should have. But another part of him felt the need to prove himself. He didn't want Tipper to think he wasn't smart. He wanted Tipper to like him. So he determined he would show Tipper he was wrong.

> *The way Tipper looked at Bramble embarrassed him.*

"We are clever," Bramble protested.

"If you say so, Bramble. I'll tell you what. I could use a clever friend like you right now. Wanna' hang out?"

Bramble was kind of surprised Tipper wanted to hang out after he'd made fun of him, but maybe he was wrong about Tipper. He decided to give him a chance. "Sure. I guess so," he said.

"Great. You know, for a clever fox, you sure need to learn a thing or two! And I'm gonna' teach you." The otter pointed toward Silver Creek. "You see that wolf

over there, by the bank?"

Bramble looked where Tipper was pointing. The wolf was sleeping in the shade of a cypress. Next to him was a basket and fishing pole. "Yeah, I see him," Bramble said.

Tipper snickered. "Now that's what I call a patsy. Watch this." Tipper crept over to where the wolf slept. He opened the basket, took out a fish, then turned to Bramble and took a bow.

This rather upset Bramble. It wasn't Tipper's fish to take. He tried to think of how to handle the situation as Tipper slinked back.

He opened the basket, took out a fish, then turned to Bramble and took a bow.

"See?" Tipper said when he'd returned. He held the fish out. "There's nothing to it. Now you try." TRUTH 1b

"No thanks!" Bramble said, waving his hands in front of him. "I don't steal things."

"It's not stealing," Tipper said. "Not exactly . . . I gave him a sporting chance. Can I help it if he's too lazy to look after his fish?"

Bramble realized then that Tipper was not the kind of friend he should be hanging around. He decided it was time to go, and was about to say goodbye when he noticed the wolf beginning to stir. Before Bramble could think to say or do anything, Tipper tossed the fish to him and said, "Since you're so clever, think up a good story," then dashed into the nearby woods.

Bramble looked at the fish in his hands, then to the woods where Tipper had disappeared, then back to the wolf, who was now awake. Everything was happening so fast, he could hardly understand what was going on.

Everything was happening so fast, he could hardly understand what was going on.

He froze as the wolf pulled himself up on all fours and stretched his body.

That's when Bramble noticed the basket. Tipper had left the lid off! The wolf would surely notice!

The wolf looked at the basket and then all around. That's when he spotted Bramble with the fish still in his hands. The wolf walked quickly to where Bramble stood with his ill-gotten gains.

"So you're not only a thief, you're a liar, too, huh?"

"What do you think you're doing, young man? Do you think this is funny?" he asked.

Bramble was paralyzed. "N-N-No, sir!"

"If you had asked me for the fish, I would have shared with you. But I won't have folks stealing the rewards of my hard work!" The wolf furrowed his brow.

"Please sir," Bramble pleaded. "It was the otter! It was Tipper!"

"What otter?" The wolf said, looking around. "All I see is you, and you are the one with my fish."

The wolf snatched the fish from the ground then stood and glared at Bramble.

"Honest, Mister Wolf, it wasn't me!" Bramble laid the fish at the wolf's feet. "Please, take the fish back. It's yours."

The wolf snatched the fish from the ground then stood and glared at Bramble. "So you're not only a thief, you're a liar, too, huh?"

It was at that moment that Bramble realized who the real patsy was. And it wasn't the wolf. He was the patsy. He was the one who had allowed himself to be tricked.

Bramble thought of what his parents had taught him. About the importance of choosing his friends wisely. He should have paid attention to the voice inside that told him Tipper wasn't the kind of friend to have. Tracker would never do something so terrible to him. Bramble began to cry. "Please, Mister Wolf! I didn't do anything! You have to believe me!" He buried his face in his hands.

It was at that moment that Bramble realized who the real patsy was.

Just then, a squirrel scurried over from a nearby tree. "Mister Wolf, the fox is telling the truth. Tipper has been causing trouble all up and down the creek. Tipper did it. He stole your fish."

Bramble used the back of his arms to wipe his tears. He looked up at the wolf, who seemed unsure of what to believe. All Bramble could do was hold his breath and hope he would see the truth in his eyes.

After several long moments of silence, the wolf spoke. "Well, I suppose it's all right. I did get my fish back. But you pick better friends and stay away from

that Tipper before he gets you in serious trouble."

"Yes, sir, Mister Wolf! I hope I never see that otter again!" Bramble said. "Thank you for believing me. And thank you, Mister Squirrel. I didn't know Tipper was that kind of friend. I didn't know he would do something like that until it was too late. I have another friend who's an otter named Willow. He's super nice. So I thought all otters were supposed to be nice."

The wolf nodded his head. "Well, everyone is supposed to be nice. But niceness is not something you're born with, it's something you choose. Let this be a lesson to you, young man. Always choose to be nice, and always choose nice friends." CREATION 2b,c

"Yes, sir. I will!" Bramble said.

And he sure meant it.

CHAPTER 10
Bramble's Burrow

One morning, when Bramble was headed out to explore the Woodlands with Tracker, his father stopped him on his way out. "Where are you going?" he asked.

"I'm going to find Tracker. I promised we could hang out today."

"Promises are important," Father Fox said, "but so is learning to survive. This morning you have a very important lesson to learn. Tracker will have to wait."

He had his heart set on spending the day with his friend.

Bramble was annoyed. He didn't want to learn a lesson. He had his heart set on spending the day with his friend. "But he'll be waiting!" he whined.

"He'll understand," Father Fox told him.

"Ah man! What do I have to learn?"

"You need to learn how to dig a proper burrow.

Spending the night in wet, cold weather is very unpleasant. And when you're ready to start a family of your own, you will need to be able to provide them with a safe place to live."

Bramble had dug many holes before. He didn't understand why he had to waste a perfectly good day digging a big hole in the dirt. And what about Tracker? He promised he would meet him at Silver Creek!

Bramble just wanted the lesson to be over.

Bramble just wanted the lesson to be over. He decided he would agree with everything his father said and not ask any questions. Hopefully that would make the lesson go by faster. Maybe he would be done fast enough to still go exploring with Tracker.

Unfortunately, it seemed Father Fox was in no hurry to get done teaching. He spoke slowly and talked about things that were not interesting to Bramble. Some of what he taught was familiar to Bramble, such as how to find south by keeping the rising sun on his left and the setting sun on his right. Other ideas such

as proper drainage and how to know which trees had too many roots were new and a little confusing. Even worse were the parts about air flow and headroom. The whole time Father Fox spoke, Bramble daydreamed of the things he and Tracker would do later.

Finally, it seemed like the lesson had come to an end. Father Fox looked Bramble in the eyes. "Any questions about what you learned?" he asked.

Bramble had plenty of questions, but he didn't want to ask them and risk another long lecture. And he didn't want his father to find out he hadn't been paying attention. "No, sir," he said.

The whole time Father Fox spoke, Bramble daydreamed of the things he and Tracker would do later.

"Okay then. Let's see how much you learned. I want you to dig a burrow. But remember, it has to pass the test."

Bramble was afraid he didn't know enough to build a proper burrow, but then he remembered that a burrow is basically just a big hole, and he'd dug plenty

of those. "Where do you want it, Father?"

"If you were paying attention, you'll know where to dig."

Bramble was a little worried, but he was more excited to get to Tracker, so he picked what he thought was a nice spot on the north side of a cedar tree. He dug and dug and then he dug some more. He dug quickly so there would be time left to explore with Tracker. The work would have gone quicker, but the cedar tree he dug near had a lot of roots that had to be chewed through and rocks that had to be plucked out.

> *He dug quickly so there would be time left to explore with Tracker.*

Father Fox watched carefully, but he said nothing. Bramble figured that meant he was doing okay.

When he finished his burrow, the floor was lumpy and the roof was low in places. All the dirt he'd dug out of the hole was sitting in big piles by the entrance. Still, it was big enough to crawl through and turn around. "How is that, Father?" he asked.

"We'll see," Father Fox said. "Digging the burrow was only half the test. You go explore with Tracker,

and we'll do the other half when you come back."

That evening, when Bramble came home, his father was waiting for him. "Okay, son. It's time to finish testing your burrow."

"But it's getting dark outside."

"I know. What better time to test a burrow?"

"If you were paying attention, you'll know where to dig."

That made Bramble a little nervous. What would the rest of the test be?

Father Fox continued. "You get to sleep in your own burrow tonight. In the morning, you can tell me if it passed the test."

Sleeping in his own burrow didn't sound so bad to Bramble. In fact, it kind of sounded like an adventure. Passing the second part of the test was going to be easy. Bramble laughed to himself as he thought of how he had outsmarted his father.

> *That made Bramble a little nervous. What would the rest of the test be?*

Bramble said goodnight, then slipped into the dark burrow feeling excited and proud, but as he moved over the lumpy floor, he frowned. "Oh goodness!" he said, as he stumbled on the ridges and bumps. "I guess I could have done a little better on this floor. I'll smooth it out in the morning when the sun comes up."

Determined to make the best of it, Bramble curled up in his cramped little space on the bare ground and tried to sleep. But after a while, the lumps and bumps

in the floor felt bigger and bigger. As he tossed and turned trying to find a comfortable position, he remembered his father saying something about digging in long, straight strokes. He imagined his family curled up comfortably in their cozy den.

As Bramble lay there, clouds covered the moon and a damp smell crept into the burrow. Bramble knew it meant rain. But at least he was safe underground.

Or so he thought.

When the rain started, a stream of water trickled into the burrow. It ran

Before long, Bramble felt cold and miserable.

through all the loose dirt he'd left at the entrance. The dirt quickly turned to mud and washed into the burrow. Because there was no pit in the floor to catch the water, all that mud ran into Bramble's bed. Before long, Bramble felt cold and miserable.

When he could take no more, he stood and made his way toward the entrance. He wanted to gather some soft moss and hay to make himself a new bed.

"Ouch!" Bramble had gotten a nasty thump right between the ears. The ceiling of his burrow was

entirely too low. To make things worse, the entrance faced north, so the wind blew straight into the tunnel, and he got a face full of cold rain. When he finally exited the burrow, he found that the moss was now wet through. "Aww man!" he said. "I should have made my bed this morning when I had the chance," he said. The more he thought about it, the fun he had playing with Tracker seemed a lot less important. As much as he didn't want to, he knew he was going to go to his father and admit he had messed up. There was no way he could stay in his burrow the rest of the night.

As much as he didn't want to, he knew he was going to go to his father and admit he had messed up.

Bramble walked into the family den. His ears were tucked, his tail dragged the ground behind him. He was ashamed, but he had no choice. He was cold, wet, and completely miserable.

He found his father and mother were awake. It seemed they were expecting him.

His mother opened her arms to him. "Come to me and get warm," she said.

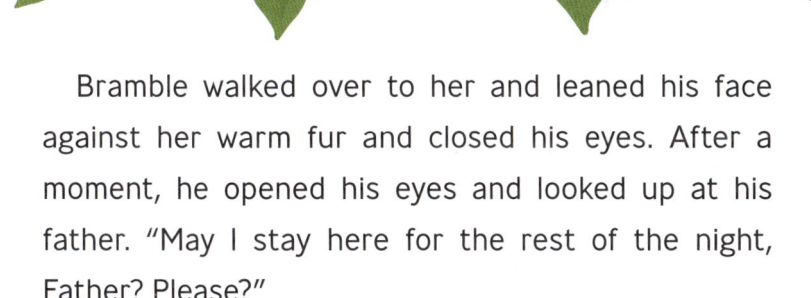

Bramble walked over to her and leaned his face against her warm fur and closed his eyes. After a moment, he opened his eyes and looked up at his father. "May I stay here for the rest of the night, Father? Please?"

Father Fox looked down at him and smiled, "This is still your home, Bramble; you're always welcome here. But tell me one thing first. Did your burrow pass the test?"

He found his father and mother were awake. It seemed they were expecting him.

Bramble looked down at the floor. "No sir."

"And did you learn anything?"

"Yes, sir. I should have paid attention to you. I just wanted to play with Tracker, but I know now that you were just trying to teach me something far more important." TRUTH Ic

Father Fox walked over to Bramble, gave him a tight hug, then pulled back and looked him in the eyes. "You have passed the test, son."

"But I did such a horrible job. I ignored you, and my burrow was awful!"

BRAMBLE'S BURROW 85

"You're absolutely right, son. You did a bad job digging a burrow, but you did a good job humbling yourself. And I bet next time you will pay much better attention and follow directions. Am I right?"

"Yes sir. I will."

"As soon as the ground dries off, we'll try digging again," Father Fox told him. "And this time I want to see both eyes watching and both ears listening. Deal?"

"Deal." Bramble sighed deeply. "I'm sorry, Dad. It won't happen again."

Father Fox cuddled him. "I know, son. Now let's get some sleep."

CHAPTER II
Bramble and Fletch

Bramble couldn't believe he was going to visit the inside of Mister Ranger's cabin. It seemed like everyone had been there but him. And each one had a different story to tell. Bramble's sister Star told him about a squeaky bed for sleeping and how high it made her bounce. Tracker told him about a radio in the office named Roger. One that didn't play music, but instead talked back when you spoke to it.

And now it was his turn to find something new. A story all his own.

When Mister Ranger opened the cabin door to him and Mother Fox, he opened the door to a new and exciting world. Even before he stepped inside, Bramble smelled, heard, and saw things that were beyond anything he could imagine.

It seemed like everyone had been there but him.

Mister Ranger touched a switch on the wall, and

suddenly the dark room brightened as if he'd let in the sun. The ground was covered in softness and there were tables and chairs and coat racks and all kinds of things Mister Ranger had to explain. There was a radio on one of the tables playing music, and, on the ceiling, a fan that made wind blow. The entire space was full of curiosities and surprise.

Some of Mister Ranger's curious things were actually quite practical. Mister Ranger served Bramble and his mother food out of a metal can and water that came from a pipe. Afterward, Bramble was so full, he became a bit sleepy, so he hunted for the mysterious squeaky bed.

He wasn't going to jump on it. Mother Fox had already given him a stern warning about that. He was going to curl up on it for a little nap.

The bed was as wonderful as Star said it would be. Bramble hopped on top of it and was about to settle into one of the fluffy white pillows when he heard something strange. He looked around for the source of the noise. A hawk! Perched on a stand in the corner.

"Oh! You're a hawk!" Bramble said.

The bird looked at him. "All day, every day," he said.

Bramble found it strange to see a hawk in a house with a roof and no space to fly. But, then again, foxes didn't really belong indoors either. "Do you live here?" he asked. STEWARDSHIP 5b

The hawk shifted on his perch. "For the moment. I'm staying here until my wing heals."

"I'm staying here until my wing heals."

"Oh. Does it hurt?"

"Only when I move it," the hawk said. "My name is Fletcher, but you can call me Fletch."

"Hi, Fletch. My name is Bramblewood, but you can call me Bramble."

Bramble was sad to leave his new friend, but he promised to come back and visit.

Fletch laughed. "I always wonder why parents give their children long names when they're just going to call them something shorter."

Bramble nodded. "I know why. It's so we know when we're in trouble," he said, then imitated his mother's voice calling him: "Bramblewood, come here this instant!"

The two laughed, knowing it was true.

"You're right. When my mother calls me 'Fletcher,' I know she wants my full attention!"

"Exactly," Bramble agreed.

Fletch and Bramble talked on and on until Mother Fox came in and said it was time to go. Bramble was

sad to leave his new friend, but he promised to come back and visit.

After that day, he made a point of coming by Mister Ranger's as much as possible. He wanted to be sure Fletch wasn't lonely. The hawk always seemed to brighten when he came. He told Bramble story after thrilling story, like about flying up to the clouds and standing on mountaintops. He told the stories so well, he made Bramble feel like he was there himself.

> *After that day, he made a point of coming by Mister Ranger's as much as possible.*

One day, instead of telling his own stories, Fletch asked Bramble to tell him a story about something exciting foxes do.

Bramble thought and thought, but, compared to the stories Fletch told, nothing about being a fox seemed exciting or worth telling. "There's nothing exciting about being a fox," Bramble said.

"How about when you dig holes in the ground to live in," Fletch said. "That could be exciting."

"They're not holes, they're burrows," Bramble

corrected. "There's a difference."

Fletch laughed. "Okay, so what's the difference?"

"A hole in the ground is rough and cold and fills up with water when it rains. A burrow is dark and quiet like a hole, but it is just the right size, the floor is smooth, and it doesn't smell funny. And it keeps out the rain and wind. But what I like most about my burrow is that my family lives there."

Fletch spread his wings. "That sounds nice, but you're right. Not very exciting. Have you had any adventures?"

Mister Ranger walked in about that time. "Tell Fletch about the time you fell down the well," he suggested.

"Oh yeah!" Bramble said. Then he told Fletch the whole tale from beginning to end. Fletch sat fascinated, and Bramble could tell that the hawk found this story very exciting.

The next time Bramble came by to visit, Mister Ranger told him Fletch was gone. His wing had healed, so it was time for him to leave.

"He's outside where he can fly again. The clouds and treetops are his home, and he misses them when he's down here," Mister Ranger explained.

Bramble was sad. He knew this day would come, but he hadn't expected it to be so soon. He realized he wasn't ready to lose his new friend.

"Will I ever see him again?" he asked.

"Yes, but he will see you more than you see him.

Bramble was sad. He knew this day would come, but he hadn't expected it to be so soon.

And when he does, he will remember what a good friend you were. Don't worry, Bramble. Time passes and seasons change, but true friendship lasts forever."

Mister Ranger was right. And now he had his own story to tell about Mister Ranger's cabin. A story no one else had. He hadn't made the bed springs squeak or spoken to Roger the Radio, but he'd done something even better. He'd found a friendship that would last forever. And that was the most exciting story of all.

CHAPTER 12
The Angry Spot

Even the smallest spot of anger can be a lot like an itch just out of reach. If not dealt with, that tiny bit of anger can turn into something much bigger. Bramble's tiny spot of anger toward Tipper the Otter was beginning to grow.

Bramble found it very hard to forgive Tipper. Not only had he stolen a fish from Mister Wolf, but he'd gotten Bramble into a whole heap of trouble doing it. If it hadn't been for Mister Squirrel, who knows what would have happened! CREATION 2b,c

> *Bramble found it very hard to forgive Tipper.*

Bramble often thought about that day and wondered if Tipper ever got punished for what he did. He resented that he never had a chance to tell him what a terrible thing he'd done. The more Bramble thought of it, the angrier he became. Finally, when he could stand it no

94 FRIENDS OF THE WOODLANDS TRAIL

longer, he decided to confront the otter.

Bramble went to the spot where it all happened. Mister Wolf happened to be there, fishing from under the same shade tree by the creek.

"Excuse me, Mister Wolf," he said, "have you seen Tipper the Otter?"

The wolf turned to look at him, then shook his head. "I thought you learned your lesson, young man."

"Its about time Tipper learned his lesson, too!"

"I did," Bramble said, "and it's about time Tipper learned his lesson, too!"

"I see," the wolf said. "Tipper lives in a burrow farther up the bank, right next to the bent oak tree."

Bramble thanked the wolf then went on his way.

As luck would have it, Bramble found Tipper sitting on the bank in front of the bent oak tree. He stomped over to the otter. "Hey, Tipper. Remember me? The patsy?" Bramble was ready for a battle. But when Tipper turned to look at him, the otter's face was wet with tears. All the things Bramble had planned to say went away.

"Oh, it's you," Tipper said, then turned back and hung his head.

Bramble found it hard to be angry when Tipper was so upset. "What's wrong?" he asked.

"My Dad is very sick," Tipper explained, wiping his face with a paw. "Momma told me to pray, but I've been so bad, I know God won't listen to my prayers. He's gonna' die, and it will be all my fault." PROVIDENCE 6a,b,c

Bramble hadn't expected this. He knew what Tipper was saying didn't sound right, but he didn't know what to say to make things better. "You'd better come talk with my father. He'll know what to do."

> *"You'd better come talk with my father. He'll know what to do."*

Tipper straightened and turned back to look at him. "Really? You'd let me talk to him?"

"Of course. You need help, and I think he can give it to you."

"I'll try anything," Tipper said, then stood and followed Bramble to his home.

When they found Father Fox outside the burrow, Tipper told him about his sick father, but he also told

*Father Fox listened quietly the whole time
the otter talked.*

him about skipping chores, telling lies, and taking things that didn't belong to him. He even told him about leaving Bramble with the stolen fish. Bramble saw more tears building up in Tipper's eyes when he said he was afraid God wouldn't listen to his prayers because of all the bad things he'd done.

Father Fox listened quietly the whole time the otter talked. When Tipper finished, he was silent a bit longer before he spoke.

"It seems to me that when you have done something wrong, you need prayer more than ever," he began. "But God understands your father needs help right now, and that you'll try to be a better boy tomorrow."

> *"It seems to me that when you have done something wrong, you need prayer more than ever."*

Tipper nodded, and the tears slipped from his eyes. "What should I say to God? I'm not good at saying prayers."

"You just tell God how you feel. Tell him what you've done and what you need. Just like you've done with me."

"And do you think He'll listen?" Tipper asked.

FRIENDS OF THE WOODLANDS TRAIL

"I know He will," Father Fox answered.

Tipper smiled and dried his eyes. He thanked Bramble and Father Fox for everything, then said he needed to get back to help his mother.

After he left, Bramble thought about the nasty trick Tipper had played on him. He hadn't liked being the patsy, but somehow the thought of it didn't make him as angry this time. Bramble decided to pray.

"Please, God, help Tipper's father get well, and help Tipper be a better friend, so he can have more of them."

Two days later, Bramble ran into Tipper at the creek. Tipper was smiling, and when he saw Bramble, he grabbed a large fish from the pile next to him and ran over.

"Hi, Bramble! I have something for you to take to you father."

Brambles shook his head. "Have you been dry fishing again, Tipper?"

"No way! My dry fishing days are over. I caught it myself," he said, proudly. "Would you take it to your father and tell him I said thanks . . . for everything?"

Bramble smiled. "Sure I will," he said, then remem-

bered his prayer. "So how is your father?"

"He's a little better," Tipper said. "I think he will heal completely in time. But I ask God every day to make it soon. I've been talking to God a lot lately. It helps me remember to make right choices. Like I promised." TRUTH Ib

"That's great, Tipper," Bramble said, and then he had an idea. "Hey! Maybe you and I can go fishing sometime."

"That would be awesome!" Tipper said, then he looked down and kicked at the pebbles in the dirt. "You know, the truth is, I don't really have any friends. I've played so many tricks, no one wants to hang out with me anymore."

"Well, I do," Bramble said. "As long as you never try to make me the patsy again."

Tipper laughed. "Deal."

Bramble was glad to know that Tipper's dad was going to be all right. He was also glad to know that Tipper was going to be all right. And when he was sure he had forgiven Tipper, he knew he was going to be all right, too.

CHAPTER 13
The Long Walk

Bramble was out exploring near Crown Hill. On the trail, he found a box turtle trudging along slowly. "Hey, Mister Turtle. Wanna' race?" Bramble joked.

"Sure. How about I race you home?"

Bramble smiled. "I was only kidding," he said. "A race between a fox and a turtle wouldn't be very fair."

"I should say not," the turtle said, then quickly pulled his head and legs inside his shell. After a second, he peeked his head back out and said, "I win!" then laughed so hard he almost flipped over on his shell.

"Hey, that's not fair!" Bramble said, his eyebrows pulling together.

"I told you," Mister Turtle said. "I may be slow, but I can always get home in a hurry."

Bramble opened his mouth to protest, but was distracted when a flash of color passed in front of him. It was a butterfly that had come to rest on a nearby

tree branch. He'd never seen one like it, and he was totally entranced until he heard a voice call his name.

"Hello, Bramble!" the voice said.

Bramble looked. The voice seemed to be coming from the tree, but in all his life, he'd never known a talking butterfly.

"You sure do have a big voice for a little butterfly," Bramble said. "But how did you know my name?"

The voice laughed. "No, silly. It's me! Up here."

Bramble looked higher in the tree and saw a hawk perched on a high branch. "Fletch! It's you!"

Fletch laughed. "I have a surprise for you," he said.

"All day, every day!" he said.

"What are you doing up there?"

Fletch laughed. "I have a surprise for you," he said.

"What is it?"

"I'll have to show you."

"Where is it?"

"I'll have to take you there," Fletch said, then winked.

Fletch had to hop along for Bramble to keep up with him. It was a lot of work for him, but it was also a lot of work for Bramble. The path Fletch took him on was all uphill!

Bramble was soon out of breath. "This better be worth it," he huffed.

"Don't worry. It will be," Fletch assured him.

The path Fletch took him on was all uphill!

After several more minutes of hopping and trudging, Bramble was ready to quit. "How much farther?" he whined.

"Not much farther now," Fletch said. "We are going to the top."

"All the way to the top?" Bramble asked.

"Yes. All the way to the top," Fletch said. "Anything less, and you'll miss the surprise."

Bramble turned around and looked back the way he'd come. All the animals looked like tiny ants. He couldn't believe he'd come so far.

"Are you sure this is gonna' be worth it," Bramble

asked. "You know I'm gonna' have to walk back down, right?"

"Yes, Bramble," Fletch said, rolling his eyes. "I promise. It'll be worth it."

When Bramble finally pulled himself over the last ledge, he caught his breath, then looked up at Fletch. "Now what is it you want to show me?"

Fletch continued hopping forward. "Right past these bushes," he said. "What I'm about to show you is better than my best stories. Just a few more steps."

Bramble followed Fletch through a line of bushes. When he'd pushed through the last branches, he witnessed the most awesome thing he'd ever seen. A drop-off overlooking a deep valley below. Down in the valley was a lake and a stream and buildings and a whole lot of room to run and play. It was a camp!

CREATION 2a

"Well, Bramble? Was it worth it?"

Bramble couldn't even answer. It had been worth every single step. He couldn't believe he'd never heard about it before.

The hawk nodded. "This is the way I see the world when I fly," he said. "I see things like this all the time,

but it's much better when I share them with a friend."

"It's incredible," Bramble said. "I can't wait to show Tracker!"

There were no words to describe how wonderful it was.

THE LONG WALK 105

"I knew you'd like it," Fletch said. "I have to go now, but I will see you again soon. Goodbye, friend."

Bramble waved. "Goodbye, Fletch."

"I see things like this all the time, but it's much better when I share them with a friend."

Bramble thought about how wonderful it must be to see the world the way Fletch did. To feel the wind fluttering through your wings and know there was no limit to the places you could go or the things you could see.

Bramble stayed there for a while daydreaming until it was time to head home. On his way down, he walked through grass and flowers, but he pretended he was soaring through the winds and clouds.

CHAPTER 14
Tracker in Charge

Tracker and his family were sunning themselves outside their cave one morning when Mister Owl swooped in. He looked nervous and upset, and he spoke very quickly. "Hoot! Hoot! Big news! Big news! We need your help! Hoot!"

Father and Mother Lion jumped to their feet. "What is it, Mister Owl?" Father asked.

"Old Moe is sick. He needs your help. No one knows how to use the Woodland's plants as medicine like you two. Please, come quickly. Hoot!" STEWARDSHIP 5b

"Yes, we'll come right away," Father Lion said.

But there was a problem. "What will we do about Tracker and Violet?" Mother Lion asked. "Old Moe lives so far. The kids can't run that distance without taking many breaks."

"Tracker is old enough to watch his little sister," Father Lion assured her, then turned to Tracker. "Son, you'll

be the man of the house while we're gone, won't you?"

FAMILY 4a

Tracker stood and held his head high. "Yes, sir!"

Mother Lion walked to Tracker and gave him a kiss between the ears. "You are growing up so fast," she told him. "But we will probably be gone all day. We may not even be home until after you two have gone to bed. Are you sure you can handle that?"

"Son, you'll be the man of the house while we're gone, won't you?"

Tracker rested his head against his mother. "I won't let you down, Mom."

"We know you won't, son," Father Lion said. "But there is one very important rule. You two can play right outside our cave, but don't go anywhere else."

"We won't. I promise."

Tracker watched his parents take off, Mister Owl leading the way from above. Being left in charge made Tracker feel grown.

He and Violet went inside the cave. At first they played games. Tracker let Violet choose the games they would play. He took pride in caring for her needs,

108 FRIENDS OF THE WOODLANDS TRAIL

feeding her when she was hungry, and helping her find activities to pass the time. Tracker was enjoying his new role as man of the house.

But as the day dragged on, Tracker became restless. He was bored of the games his sister chose. The cave felt smaller by the minute, and he kept thinking of how good it would feel to run free through the Woodlands. Then he remembered his promise to his parents and sighed hopelessly.

> *The cave felt smaller by the minute, and he kept thinking of how good it would feel to run free through the Woodlands.*

Tracker decided some fresh air might do some good, so he took Violet outside to play. He made sure she stayed close to the cave, like Father Lion had said. But after a while, even being outside made him feel like a prisoner.

Then Willow the Otter dropped by. Tracker was relieved to see him. Maybe a friend could cure his boredom.

"Willow!" Tracker said. "I'm glad you came. I've been so bored!"

"Hey, Tracker. A bunch of us guys are going out fishing. Grab your rod. Let's go!"

Tracker couldn't believe his bad luck. This couldn't be happening! He thought seeing his friend would make the day better. Instead, he felt worse than ever.

"I can't go. I'm taking care of Violet."

110 FRIENDS OF THE WOODLANDS TRAIL

He was going to miss out on all the fun!

"You've gotta' be kidding me!" Tracker said, smacking his paw to his forehead. He shook his head. "I can't go. I'm taking care of Violet."

"That's too bad. My father got me this new fishing rod. I wanted you to help me test it out."

Things just kept getting worse and worse. He couldn't miss this. He just couldn't! Tracker thought a moment. If he was careful, and kept an eye on Violet, maybe he could take his sister to the creek with him, and his parents would never have to know. What harm could it do? They'd let him take Violet out lots of times before. CREATION 2b,c

If he was careful, and kept an eye on Violet, maybe he could take his sister to the creek with him.

Tracker made up his mind. "Wait right here, Willow," he said, then, turning to his sister, "Get your things, Violet. We're going fishing," then he dashed into the cave and reappeared at record speed.

The three made their way to Silver Creek. Tracker noticed a queasy feeling in his stomach, like some-

TRACKER IN CHARGE | 111

thing wasn't right. The farther he got from home, the worse it got. He forced himself to ignore it, though. This fishing trip was going to be too great to miss.

Many of their friends were already gathered at the creek when they arrived. Tracker and Willow got started right away, finding worms, baiting their hooks, and throwing out their lines. Tracker quickly lost track of time. He did his best to keep a close eye on Violet, but he forgot a couple of times and had to look for her. She was never too far away.

By the end of the day, they'd all caught plenty of fish. When some of Tracker's friends said they had to go home, he realized how late it had gotten. His parents might come home soon! If they got there before him, they'd know he'd broken the rules. It wouldn't matter if both he and Violet were safe, he'd be in big trouble. Tracker quickly gathered his things, said goodbye to his friends, and told Violet it was time to go.

As they walked, Tracker thought about how well he'd done as the man of the house. Violet was in the same shape his parents left her in, and he'd caught five trout—big ones—to feed himself and Violet for dinner. After they ate, he and Violet got ready for bed

and were asleep in no time.

When Tracker woke the next morning, he found both his parents preparing breakfast. Violet woke shortly after, and they all sat down to eat.

"Old Moe is already feeling better," Mother Lion said. "And, Tracker, it seems you did a great job looking after your sister while we were gone. I'm very proud of you."

Tracker instantly felt that same queasiness he'd gotten in his stomach when he went fishing. He knew his mother wouldn't be saying those things if she knew the truth.

Every moment he kept the secret was making him feel worse.

"I told you he would," Father Lion said. "He's very responsible, just like his old dad."

Tracker smiled, but he felt terrible.

At first he was afraid Violet would tell his parents what they'd done. But she didn't. Still, the queasiness wouldn't go away. He'd gotten away with the fishing trip, but he'd lied to his parents, and every moment he kept the secret was making him feel worse.

Tracker couldn't take it anymore. It was awful, like

someone was playing the drums inside him. He didn't care if he got in trouble. This feeling was worse than any punishment he could think of.

Tracker looked up from his plate, and let it all out in one breath.

> *Tracker looked up from his plate, and let it all out in one breath.*

"Willow came over yesterday, and all our friends were at the creek, and he had a new fishing pole, and I was so bored, and I'm sorry. I'm really sorry. I'll never do it again. I feel awful." Tracker hung his head in shame.

Mother and Father Lion were silent. They looked at each other and then back at Tracker. It felt like forever.

Finally, Father Lion spoke.

"Son, it took a lot of courage to tell the truth. You might have gotten away with it if you hadn't told us."

Tracker looked up at his father. "But I didn't get away with it. I didn't get away with it in here," he said, placing his paw on his stomach. "I've felt sick inside. I thought the feeling would go away, but it hasn't. It's just gotten worse."

"That's a terrible feeling, son," Father Lion said. "It's called guilt."

Tracker hung his head again.

Father Lion continued, "I left you here as a leader. But the first person you needed to lead was yourself. You have a conscience that tells you right from wrong. But you have to choose to listen to it and choose to do right."

Tracker slumped lower in his chair. "I guess you'll never leave me in charge again as long as I live," he said.

"On the contrary," Father Lion said. "You have to learn to handle responsibility. You have to practice making the right choices. I will leave you in charge again, and this time I have no doubt you'll make the right choices."

Tracker sat up straight. He didn't want to disappoint his father again. He would practice listening to his conscience and choosing right. "I will, Dad. I really will," he said.

And he meant it.

CHAPTER 15
The Cookout

Bramble and Tracker were headed out to East Meadow when Bramble noticed something wonderful in the air.

"Do you smell that?" he asked.

They found Mister Ranger outside his cabin flipping hamburgers on the grill.

Tracker held his nose high and sniffed a couple of times. "Wow! I sure do!" he said. "What is that? Yum!"

"I think it's coming from Mister Ranger's cabin," Bramble said. "Let's go!"

They found Mister Ranger outside his cabin flipping hamburgers on the grill. The sweetest-smelling smoke rose around him.

"Howdy, Mister Ranger. Whatcha' doin'?" Tracker asked, trying to sound innocent.

Mister Ranger laughed. "What do you think I'm doing, Tracker?"

"Looks like you're cooking some of the best-smelling, most terrific burgers on the planet," Tracker said. "You must be the best hamburger maker ever. Don't you wanna' share with your good friends Tracker and Bramble? Huh?" Tracker winked.

Mister Ranger shook his head and laughed again. "Oh, all right!" he said. "But don't blame me if you're too full to eat your supper!"

Tracker and Bramble were each given a hamburger. They were not the same size, though.

Tracker and Bramble were each given a hamburger. They were not the same size, though. When Bramble noticed his was smaller, he was upset. "That's not fair! Tracker's is bigger," he said. CREATION 2b,c

Mister Ranger frowned. "I know, Bramble. But it wouldn't be nice if yours and Tracker's were the same size. His is bigger because he's bigger. If you ate as much as Tracker, you'd get sick."

This explanation did not make Bramble feel better.

He felt cheated. He ate his burger, but he didn't enjoy it. He was too busy sulking.

He and Tracker finished their burgers, said goodbye

When Bramble noticed his was smaller, he was upset.

118　FRIENDS OF THE WOODLANDS TRAIL

to Mister Ranger, then headed in the direction of East Meadow. Bramble walked with his chin drooped to his chest. He saw Tracker peeking at him every once in a while.

"What do you want to do when we get to the meadow?" Tracker asked.

"I don't feel much like playing," Bramble said, keeping his head low. "I think I'm gonna' go home now," he said, then turned and ran home without another word to his friend.

He ate his burger, but he didn't enjoy it.

When Bramble got to the burrow, Father Fox and his sister Star were there. "I'm glad you came home early," his father said. "You and your sister have chores to do today."

Bramble's ears pulled back and his tail drooped, losing all its fluff. "Not chores!" he whined. He'd forgotten he had to bring in fresh herbs and straw to make a clean bed for his family. Usually this wouldn't bother him since Star had to do her chores, too. But he was still upset about what had happened at Mister

Ranger's. He didn't want to do chores. All he really wanted to do was lie around and feel sorry for himself.

Star walked over to him. "Bramble, you don't have to make the bed if you don't want to. I can do it."

"You would do that?" he asked.

"Sure I would. You're my brother."

He felt guilty when he thought of how he'd acted.

Bramble looked at Star. She was being so kind. It wouldn't be fair if she had to do all the chores. But Bramble was glad she had offered, so he accepted. "You know what, sis? You're all right. Thanks a bunch!"

Bramble realized how blessed he was to have a sister like Star, who didn't insist on fairness. TRUTH Ic

Suddenly, Bramble realized he hadn't been that way with Tracker or Mister Ranger. He felt guilty when he thought of how he'd acted. Bramble wanted to tell them he was sorry, but he was afraid they'd be too upset with him. He decided to talk to his father about what had happened.

Father Fox listened to Bramble's story.

"Why do you think Mister Ranger gave Tracker more than he gave me?" Bramble asked. "Do you think he likes Tracker better?"

"Not at all, Bramble. Tracker is bigger than you," Father Fox said. "Fairness is nice, but sometimes kindness is even better."

"I guess," Bramble said.

"Think about it," his father continued. "Do you think Mister Ranger was being fair when he shared his burgers with you or do you think he was being kind?" he asked Bramble.

"He was being kind."

"That's right, son. Because you hadn't done anything to earn the burgers. And Mister Ranger didn't have to share with you. But it was sure nice of him to do it. And I bet you were glad he did."

"I guess you're right."

"If he were being fair, he would have asked you to do him a favor in return, right? Wouldn't that have been fair?"

Bramble had not thought about it like that before. It made him feel even worse for the way he'd acted.

He had been ungrateful when he should have been thankful. He'd have to do something to make it right.

"What should I tell Tracker and Mister Ranger?" he asked. "I wasn't very nice to them."

"Why don't you try saying 'I'm sorry?' Those words can work wonders when you really mean them."

Father Fox was right. Bramble knew what he had to do. He hurried to find Tracker, hoping he could still catch him in East Meadow.

> *He had been ungrateful when he should have been thankful.*

When he reached the meadow, he was thankful to find Tracker was there. He ran to him, anxious to apologize, but Tracker spoke before he could say anything. "There you are, Bramble! I wanted to tell you I'm sorry I didn't let you have the bigger burger. I could tell it meant a lot to you, so I should have traded. Your friendship means more to me than a hamburger any day."

Now Bramble felt even worse. Tracker was such a good friend, and he had shown him such unkindness. "No, Tracker. I'm sorry," he said. "Mister Ranger was

right. It wouldn't have been nice to give you the same size as me. I'm much smaller than you."

"That's okay, Bramble," Tracker said, then stuck out his paw for Bramble to shake. "Still friends?"

Bramble grabbed Tracker's paw and gave it one big pump. "Still friends." He smiled. He felt so much better already. But there was still more to do. "You're the best, Tracker," he said, "but I have to go now," then dashed off toward Mister Ranger's cabin.

Tracker was such a good friend, and he had shown him such unkindness.

Mister Ranger was still outside when Bramble arrived. He was in a rocking chair with his feet resting on an old tree stump. His eyes were closed and it looked like he was sleeping, so Bramble slowed his pace and moved quietly across the yard.

"Excuse me, Mister Ranger?" he said when he was close, careful not to scare him.

Mister Ranger peeked one eye open. When he saw Bramble, he sat up, set his feet on the ground, and rested his elbows on his knees. "Hello there, young sir. What can I do for ya'?"

"I'm sorry, Mister Ranger. I was rude and ungrateful," Bramble said. "You didn't have to share your burgers with us, but you did. Because you're a good friend."

"Oh, that's all right, Bramble. We all make mistakes. But I'm proud of you for realizing it, and even more proud that you came and apologized. That tells me you're growing up." Mister Ranger smiled at Bramble and tousled the fur between his ears. "I'm lucky to have a friend like you."

"Wow. Thanks, Mister Ranger. That means a lot coming from you. I have to go now, but I'll see you soon."

"All right, little fella. See ya' soon," Mister Ranger said, leaning back in his chair and throwing his feet up on the stump again.

Bramble waved to Mister Ranger over his shoulder as he ran away. He had to hurry home. No time to waste. He had left Star alone to do the chores, and he was anxious to get back and help before she finished.

It was only fair that he did.

CHAPTER 16
A Sure Sign

Bramble and Tracker were walking along the banks of Silver Creek. They liked to walk there because it was a great place to meet new animals and hear the latest news.

A large whitetail deer with a stately rack of antlers was having a drink when they passed.

"Hello, Oakley!" Tracker said.

The buck turned. "Oh, hello there, Tracker. Hello, Bramble. Nice day for a stroll."

Bramble looked at Tracker "A stroll?" he asked, as they walked on. "What's that?"

"Stroll is just another word for a walk."

Bramble shook his head. "Well, why didn't he just say that then?"

Around a bend in the creek, some otters were having a splash party. It made no sense to Bramble that the game was to see who could splash the others

the most since they were all up to their necks in water. Still, they seemed to be having a great time.

Bramble spotted Willow and waved to him, "Hey there, Willow."

Willow turned and looked. "Hey, guys! Come on in for a dip!"

"Maybe later," Bramble said. "We're taking a . . . stroll," he said, eyeing Tracker. The fact that he'd learned a new word tickled Bramble. Tracker just shook his head.

> *The fact that he'd learned a new word tickled Bramble. Tracker just shook his head.*

Next, they saw Mister Wolf. He was pulling his third catch out of the water. "Hello, young fellas," he said to the boys, as he laid the fish in the pile with the other two. "Come to do some fishing?"

"Not this time," Tracker said.

"Yeah. Maybe later," Bramble said. "We're out for a stroll."

Tracker looked at Bramble and rolled his eyes. "Are you going to say that word all day?"

Bramble beamed proudly. "Yup! Sure am!"

Just past a gathering of cypress trees, the two came upon a young raccoon sitting on the bank, facing the water. He had a small pile of sticks next to him, which he was breaking into smaller pieces, one by one, and throwing them into the water. Then he would watch them float downstream.

"Hey, Tracker. Have you ever done that?" Bramble asked.

"Sure. Everybody has," Tracker said.

"Well I've never done it. But I'm going to now," Bramble said, then walked over to the raccoon. "Hi, I'm Bramble, and this is my friend Tracker. Mind if we throw in some sticks, too?" he asked.

Bramble thought maybe the raccoon was so focused, he hadn't heard him.

The raccoon didn't answer or even look at Bramble. In fact, he kept his head turned the other way, watching his sticks float downstream.

Bramble thought maybe the raccoon was so

focused, he hadn't heard him. So he spoke loudly. "Hello!" he said.

Still no response.

Bramble didn't know what to think. He'd never had someone treat him so rudely. But he would not be ignored. So he tapped the raccoon on the shoulder. As soon as he touched him, the raccoon moved away quickly, as if frightened, and turned toward Bramble, his eyes wide.

"There," Bramble said, placing his paws on his hips. "That's more like it."

The raccoon began motioning wildly with his hands and shaking his head, but he still didn't say a word. What is with this guy?

Then Bramble heard a voice behind him.

"Don't be upset with Bucky!"

Bramble turned to look. A grown-up raccoon was moving quickly his way, waving at him and Tracker.

"Hi. I'm Bucky's mom," she said. "Don't be upset if he's not answering you. Bucky is deaf."

Bramble had no idea what deaf meant, but he was afraid to ask, so he just looked at Mother Raccoon,

hoping she would explain.

"This happens all the time," she continued. "He doesn't mean to ignore you."

"What's wrong with him?" Tracker asked, looking as confused as Bramble felt.

Instead of answering, Mother Raccoon looked at Bucky and began waving her hands around wildly, too. First she patted her chest, then ran her paws down the side of her face and held them out as if offering a gift. Next she pointed to Bramble and Tracker.

"Bucky can't hear anything. He's deaf."

Bucky smiled and looked at Bramble and Tracker, then began more of the same gesturing. Finally, Bucky's mom nodded, then looked back at the boys. "Bucky can't hear anything. He's deaf."

"What is that he does with his hands? What does it mean?" Bramble asked.

"That's how deaf animals communicate. It's called sign language," she explained. "He just said that he's sorry; he didn't see you standing there."

Well that explained why Bucky ignored him. But now Bramble had so many other questions. How had Bucky become deaf? How did he learn sign language? Were there other animals who were deaf? Could he ever become deaf, too?

Bramble looked at Bucky, then back at his mother. "I'm sorry Bucky can't hear," he said. "Does it make him sad?"

Mother Raccoon smiled and shook her head, "Not at all. Bucky is very happy. We talk to each other using sign language, and he does all the things most young boys do," she said. "The only bad part is, he doesn't have many friends because they don't know how to communicate with him. So Bucky spends a lot of time alone or with me." HUMAN DIGNITY 3 a,b

"Oh," Bramble said.

Bramble and Tracker stayed a while longer and talked to Bucky with the help of his mother. It turned out, Bucky was a real nice kid, and he taught Bramble everything he knew about racing sticks down a creek.

Later that day, back at the den, Mother Fox was arranging the new bedding Star had collected. As she worked, she hummed a tune. It had been one of

Bramble's favorites when he was younger. One she would sing to him before bed. Bramble always liked to hear his mother sing. Not just because she had a nice voice, but because her happiness had a way of spreading to him through her songs.

Just then it occurred to Bramble that Bucky had never heard his mother sing. He had never even heard her voice.

"Mom," the little fox said, "Why can't some folks hear anything?"

Mother Fox stopped her work and looked at Bramble. "What makes you ask?"

"Oh, no reason," Bramble said. "It's just . . . it must be awful to never hear someone sing, or hear the crickets chirp at night, or anything ever."

"I don't know, dear," Mother Fox said. "Does it worry you?"

"No," Bramble started. "I don't know . . . maybe."

Mother Fox smiled and walked over to Bramble. She rubbed a paw over his cheek. "As much as I enjoy your inquisitive mind, I don't think that's something you need to be worried about."

"Yeah. I guess you're right. It's nothing. I was just thinking," Bramble said.

"Well promise me you'll never stop doing that."

"Yes, ma'am," Bramble said, then went out for a walk. He needed to think some more and his favorite trail was where he did his best thinking.

He wondered if not having any friends to talk to made Bucky sad.

Bramble had hoped talking about deafness would make him feel better, but he just ended up with more questions. He wondered if not having any friends to talk to made Bucky sad. He wondered if Bucky may one day be able to hear, and wished there was something he could do to help. He couldn't stop thinking of all the ways not hearing would change his life.

All of these thoughts and questions made Bramble feel funny inside, and he didn't like it. So as he walked, he prayed and asked God to help him with these feelings. After a lot of walking and a lot of praying, the answer came to him. The moment it did, he took off

running to the creek where he had last seen Bucky. He didn't want to waste any more time.

It took some searching, but he finally found Bucky and his mother picking berries in the woods near the creek. He waved at Bucky and smiled, and asked Mother Raccoon if he could speak with her. She signed something to Bucky, then turned back to Bramble.

"Is everything okay, Bramble?" she asked.

"Oh, yes, ma'am. Everything's fine. I just had a question to ask," Bramble said.

"Sure. Ask away," she said.

Bramble looked down nervously at his feet, "I was wondering if, uh . . . if maybe you could teach me sign language," he said, then looked Mother Raccoon in the eyes. "That way Bucky and I could be friends."

Mother Raccoon didn't say anything at first, she just smiled and shook her head. For a second, Bramble was afraid he'd said something wrong, but then she said, "There's nothing that would make me happier."

Bramble smiled. "Can we start right now?" he asked.

Mother Raccoon laughed. "I tell you what. You come by first thing in the morning, to the spot where

Bramble had his first sign language lesson that next morning...

you met us at the creek, and we will begin your first lesson. Bucky will help, too."

Bramble was thrilled. Somehow, although he still didn't know a single word of sign language, he felt better. He thanked Mother Raccoon for agreeing to help and ran home feeling light as air. As he ran, he

thanked God for giving him the answer he needed and for his new friend Bucky. PROVIDENCE 6a,b,c

Bramble had his first sign language lesson that next morning, and he came back every morning after that, too. Before long, he was able to talk with Bucky on his own. When he felt comfortable enough, he asked Bucky some of the questions he had about being deaf, and found out that Bucky didn't think it was so bad at all.

Especially now that he had a friend like Bramble.

CHAPTER 17
A Muddy Rescue

Tracker and Bramble were sitting on the grass at Mister Ranger's one morning watching him sharpen his chainsaw. After a while, Mister Ranger looked up at the sky. "Red skies at night, sailor's delight. Red skies in the morning, sailor take warning."

Tracker went next. "Evening red and morning gray will set the traveler on his way, but evening gray and morning red will bring down rain upon his head."

Bramble looked up at the sky. "What does that mean?" he asked.

"They're poems," Tracker said.

"They're not just poems," Mister Ranger said. "They're poems that teach a lesson." He looked up at the sky again. "When the clouds are red early in the morning, like they are now, it means there will be rain."

And rain it did!

Not just a little rain, but a good old-fashioned gully washer. It rained so hard, it was hard for Bramble to see more than a few feet in front of himself.

Mister Ranger and the boys ran to the front porch to take cover. They looked out over the downpour and listened to the thundering of rain on the tin roof shed.

A few minutes later, Fletch flew in and shook his wings. "News! Big news!"

"What is it, Fletch?" Mister Ranger asked.

> *"We have trouble. The road from the guest cabin is washing out."*

"We have trouble. The road from the guest cabin is washing out."

"That is trouble," Mister Ranger said, shaking his head. "The Johnsons have a trailer out there. They won't be able to get home."

Mister Ranger let Bramble and Tracker ride in his pickup truck. It thumped hard over the bumpy roads but, for Bramble and Tracker, going on a rescue was an exciting adventure!

For Mister Ranger, the trip was a lot less exciting and a lot more work. He enjoyed doing his job, but not

when it meant getting out in the rain. But he knew the Johnsons wouldn't want to be stranded, and he was glad to help.

Halfway to the campground, they approached a trailer stuck in the road. It was the Johnsons. They must have tried to get out before the storm got too bad. One of the trailer's wheels was stuck in a deep, muddy rut.

> *"I can tell you right now this is going to take more than my tow chain to fix."*

"Uh oh," Mister Ranger said, eyeing the situation from the driver's seat. "I can tell you right now this is going to take more than my tow chain to fix."

"What will you do then?" Bramble asked.

"I'll have to lift that wheel out of the hole."

Tracker shook his head. "That's way too big. Even Old Moe couldn't pick up that trailer."

Mister Ranger chuckled. "No, no. Not with my bare hands. There's another way. Watch and learn boys."

Tracker and Bramble followed Mister Ranger out

of the truck. He sent the Johnsons into the trailer and told them he'd call them when he needed them. Then he grabbed an axe from the back of his truck and walked over to a small tree, about as big around as his arm. "This oughta' do the trick," he said.

One of the trailer's wheels was stuck in a deep, muddy rut.

Mister Ranger swung the axe at the base of the tree over and over again. With each hit, a large chunk of wood flew off.

"Look at him go!" Tracker said. "Even Mister Beaver can't cut down a tree that fast!"

Before long, the tree was knocked down and Mister Ranger had chopped all the smaller branches off as well. What was left was a long wooden pole. Bramble was impressed by the work, but he still didn't understand how a tree was going to help lift a huge trailer from a hole.

Mister Ranger knocked on the trailer door and told Mister Johnson he was ready for his help. "I need you to come outside and pile up some large stones right next to the wheel. You'll get pretty dirty, but you can clean up at my cabin."

"Can we help?" Bramble asked.

Mister Ranger smiled. "This is some pretty rough work, but if you'll say a prayer that I can get this trailer out, we sure would appreciate it." PROVIDENCE 6a,b,c

"What about me?" Tracker asked.

"You can pray that the Johnsons get home safely."

As Bramble and Tracker watched, Mister Ranger stuck one end of the wooden pole under the trailer and rested it on the rocks Mister Johnson had piled. By putting all his weight on his end of the pole, Mister Ranger did indeed lift the trailer a bit.

"Mister Johnson, get some large rocks and put them under the tire. We'll have you out of here in no time."

Bramble was very impressed. "Wow! How did you do that?"

"You have good teachers too, and if you pay attention to them, you can learn to do surprising things."

"I had some good teachers and I paid attention," Mister Ranger said. "You have good teachers too, and if you pay attention to them, you can learn to do surprising things."

The rescue took a long time and it was a lot of hard work. Mister Johnson did get wet and muddy yet, somehow, everyone had an enjoyable adventure. Tracker and Bramble were very pleased by what Mister Ranger did, but they were also glad that he practiced what to do while the weather was good so he would be ready when the weather turned bad.

A MUDDY RESCUE

CHAPTER 18
Giving Thanks

Bramble and his family were sitting outside the burrow. Mother Fox lifted her nose and sniffed the wind. "It's going to rain soon," she said. "It will be a big storm."

Mother Fox's nose had never been wrong.

Sure enough, a few minutes later, a drop hit Bramble's forehead and rolled between his eyes. It was cold and wet. Then a few more drops fell and the wind picked up speed. Father and Mother Fox got Bramble and Star into the den. There was a storm coming, but they could give thanks for their warm burrow.

Their den was a splendid place to live. It was rather old, having belonged first to Bramble's grandfather. The walls were smooth. All the lumps and bumps had been carefully scratched away and polished over the years by the passage of furry bodies. It felt just right.

Most importantly, it had been dug under the roots of a huge oak tree. The tree's roots went deep into

the earth, holding the den's walls together. It was as sturdy a home as the old oak itself.

As the wind picked up even more and the pattering of rain turned to a hard downpour, Grandfather Fox's burrowing skills could be clearly observed. The fierce winds didn't blow into the burrow, and what little bit of rain managed to get in went down into the cellar, far away from the warm, dry bed where the family had curled up to wait out the storm.

> *There was a storm coming, but they could give thanks for their warm burrow.*

At some point, the old oak began making noises as it moved under the force of the heavy winds. They were deep creaking sounds, almost like moaning, and they carried down the trunk, through the roots, and into the den walls. In some ways, the sound was comforting. Still, it was a little scary.

Star huddled closer to her mother. She trembled harder with each crack of lightening. At times there were long, deep rumbles of thunder, and Mother Fox would put her paw around Star and squeeze her tight. "My mother used to tell me that thunder is the sound

you get when clouds bump into each other," Mother Fox told her. "Don't be frightened. Try to find something happy to think about."

"At times like this, I like to think of the things that make me truly thankful," Father Fox said. "Let's all do it together. I'll go first." Father Fox thought for a moment before he continued. "I'm thankful we are all safe in our warm dry beds."

> "There are worse things than rain," Father Fox said.

"And I'm thankful for my golf ball," Bramble said. He reached under his side of the bedding where he kept the ball, and touched it. It was his favorite thing.

Mother Fox went next. "I'm thankful for all the love I'm surrounded by," she said, nuzzling Star.

"That's something we should all be thankful for," Father Fox added.

Just then, they heard a loud popping, followed by a long crackling sound, which seemed to move closer to them as it continued.

"Something's wrong," Father Fox said. "Everybody out. Now!" he shouted.

"In the rain?" Bramble asked.

"There are worse things than rain," Father Fox said. "Now move."

The four of them scrambled in the darkness of the den, but made it outside. They stepped into whipping wind and rain. Mother and Father Fox did their best to shelter the children from the storm.

"Let's get over there," Father Fox said, pointing in the direction of some nearby bushes. It was so dark they couldn't see much, but they kept close as they moved in the direction Father Fox led them.

They reached the bushes and squeezed as far under them as they could. The wind picked up again, and another long cracking sound came from the heart of the oak tree.

Lightning flashed and, for a moment, they could see clearly. The old oak, which had stood as a sentinel overlooking the Woodlands for many years, had lost its grip on the ground. It leaned at an odd angle, and there were ripping sounds as its roots were plucked from the moist earth.

Lightning flashed again. Bramble watched, terrified, as the tree fell in one final motion, ending in a

tremendous boom that shook the ground all around.

Star whimpered, trembling harder than ever.

"Daddy!" Bramble shouted. "Our home! It's gone!"

"It's okay, kids. At least we're all right," Father Fox said. "That's all that matters."

Mother and Father Fox held their children closer, and the four of them waited out the storm together under the bushes.

When the clouds finally parted and the sun peeped from behind them, Bramble and his family could see the oak lying over the entrance to the burrow they used to call home. They had lost everything they owned—including Bramble's prized golf ball. He was devastated.

> ... *the four of them waited out the storm together under the bushes.*

Father Fox gathered the family around a small seedling growing near the fallen oak. "See this new tree?" he asked them. "It won't be big tomorrow or even next month, but it will be great in God's time. And if it's lucky, maybe a family of foxes will live and

"Here in the shadow of the old tree is a new beginning. And we will have a new beginning, too."

love and laugh among its roots." PROVIDENCE 6a,b,c

Bramble thought about that for a moment. He thought about how things come and things go, and how there's nothing you could do about it.

"So you see?" Father Fox continued. "Here in the shadow of the old tree is a new beginning. And we will have a new beginning, too."

The thought comforted Bramble, and he was thankful he had such a wise father to teach him. He was also thankful that, while some things went away, his family's love would always be there.

The next day Father Fox dug a new burrow. At first it smelled too earthy, and it wasn't nearly as large as their old one. But it would keep them warm and out of the rain. Mother Fox found more soft moss to make a bed, and together they rounded out the walls as best they could. Time and furry bodies would take care of the rest.

When the four foxes settled in to their new bed that night, they gave thanks to God. This time, love and family were at the top of the list.

CHAPTER 19
Fire in the Back Grove

Bramble and Tracker were playing in the meadow one day when Bramble looked up and sniffed the air.

"What do you smell?" Tracker asked him.

"A campfire, I think," he said.

"Even your nose isn't that good," Tracker said. "We're too far from the campsites for that to be it. Maybe Mister Ranger is cooking burgers on his grill again."

Darkness was spreading over part of the sky. But it wasn't a storm cloud.

"No. That's not it," Bramble said. He looked up to see if he could tell where it was coming from. That's when he saw it. "Oh my goodness, Tracker! Look at that storm cloud!"

Tracker looked up. Darkness was spreading over part of the sky. But it wasn't a storm cloud.

"That's not a cloud, Bramble. That's smoke!" Tracker said.

Just then, Fletch the Hawk flew overhead. "Fire! Fire!" He cried from above.

"Where?" Tracker called back.

"The back grove, by the guest cabins. I can't stay. I have to go tell Mister Ranger!" he said, and then he was gone.

Days passed, and more and more word of the fire made its way to where Bramble lived

Days passed, and more and more word of the fire made its way to where Bramble lived. He heard awful stories about terrifying flames and how one of the guest cabins had burned. Most of the back grove was gone. Burnt to the ground. Many animal families had to find new homes. As they settled into other parts of the Woodlands, near where Bramble, Fletch, and Tracker lived, they shared their stories of the fire with their new neighbors.

Each story Bramble heard made him realize how blessed he was. But they also made him feel bad. His

*Just then, Fletch the Hawk flew overhead.
"Fire! Fire!" He cried from above.*

FIRE IN THE BACK GROVE 151

home was safe, but it could have just as easily been him moving to a strange new place with new faces all around.

A week passed before Bramble saw Mister Ranger. He ran across him on his favorite walking trail while out one evening for an after-dinner stroll.

"Hello, Mister Ranger. How are things?"

"Much better now that the fire is out," he said.

"What was it like?" Bramble asked. He had tried to imagine the flames burning out of control and wondered what it would have been like to see them up close.

"It was pretty bad, Bramble. One of the worst I've seen." Mister Ranger shook his head. "Many brave men fought to put it out. We lost a lot of the Woodlands, and a guest cabin, too, but things could have been much worse."

Mister Ranger looked so sad. Bramble was sad to see him like that. "Why did it have to happen?" he asked.

Mister Ranger looked Bramble in the eyes. "It didn't have to happen at all," he said. "We have rules about fire so it won't happen. But sometimes people break the rules." STEWARDSHIP 5b

This made Bramble think. Was Mister Ranger saying that if someone had only followed the rules, the fire would have never happened? All the sad stories he'd heard in the last week would have been avoided? This made Bramble angry. "Will there ever be trees and flowers there again?" he asked.

"Someday," Mister Ranger said. "When it's safe, there are people who will help plant young trees. It's been done here in the Woodlands once before, after the last fire, and now all the young trees that were planted are tall and strong. It will be pretty again, but it will take a very long time."

> *Was Mister Ranger saying that if someone had only followed the rules, the fire would have never happened?*

"And the cabin?"

"We will rebuild it."

"Is there anything I can do to help?" Bramble asked.

Mister Ranger smiled for the first time since they'd been talking. "Just keep the Woodlands in your prayers, Bramble. That's the best help I could ask for."

"I will. I promise," Bramble said. But there was something else he didn't quite understand. "I don't understand, though. If fire is such a dangerous thing, why aren't people more careful?"

Mister Ranger was quiet for a moment. "Everyone wants to have fun," he said, "but not everyone wants to be careful. But when God gives you something to enjoy, you must also take care of it." STEWARDSHIP 5b

> "Everyone wants to have fun ... but not everyone wants to be careful."

"That makes sense," Bramble said. "It's kind of like when Tracker and I helped Mister Beaver clean up the pond."

"That's right," Mister Ranger agreed. "Hopefully now you realize how important that can be. No matter how small you are, the things you do can have a big impact on the world around you."

CHAPTER 20
Little Lost Skunk

Bramble was practicing burrowing skills one evening when his sister Star returned from a walk. But she wasn't alone. She was with a young skunk.

Bramble did not like skunks. In fact, Bramble didn't know anyone who liked skunks. All Bramble knew about skunks was that they were stinky and you couldn't trust them. So why was Star bringing one home?

> *"Mother! Father! Look what I found!" Star called.*

"Mother! Father! Look what I found!" Star called. Mother and Father Fox came out of the den, and Star told them what had happened.

She had found the little skunk at the base of an elm tree, wet through and shivering cold. His name was Homer, and he was lost.

Star told them that Homer had become separated

from his parents during the rainstorm the previous morning, and had no idea how far he had come or even from what direction.

Mother Fox hurried the children inside and got Homer clean and dry, then began preparing something for him to eat. Bramble kind of felt bad for the little guy, but he didn't know why he was their problem.

Father Fox sat Homer down to talk. Bramble kept his distance, but moved close enough to hear what the skunk said. Other than his name, he didn't give Father Fox any real clues that would help. He didn't know his parents' names, just knew them as "Momma" and "Daddy," and he didn't live near any memorable landmarks he could think of. Since he'd been separated from his parents, he'd wandered from place to place, looking for someone to help.

Bramble kind of felt bad for the little guy, but he didn't know why he was their problem.

Bramble went to where his mother was preparing Homer's meal. He needed to know the plan. How long was this skunk going to be in his burrow?

"Why are we supposed to help him find his parents?" he asked her. "Do we even know any skunks?"

"We do now," Mother Fox said, then winked at Bramble. "And he will stay here until we find his family."

Bramble looked at the skunk, then back at his mother. "I'll dig him a burrow so he'll have a nice place to sleep tonight," he said.

Mother Fox shook her head. "That won't be necessary. He'll stay with us. He's lonely and very upset. He shouldn't be alone."

The thought of spending the night with a skunk upset Bramble. *How would he get any sleep? Didn't his mother care about how this would affect him?*

Father Fox walked over to Bramble and placed a hand on his shoulder. "Bramble, I want you to take Homer fishing tomorrow," he said.

"To our secret fishing hole?" Bramble asked, keeping his voice low. "Tracker would never forgive me!"

"It doesn't have to be your secret fishing hole," Father Fox said. "Just take him with you."

"But, Father. Tracker doesn't like skunks. He won't come anywhere near Homer. The otters are the same

LITTLE LOST SKUNK

way. If I take him, the kids will make fun of me."

Father Fox tightened his grip on Bramble's shoulder. "Bramblewood. Come out to the meadow with me. Now."

Bramble followed his father through the bushes. He was in big trouble for sure. His father hardly ever used his full name.

He felt bad for the way he was acting, but he couldn't help it.

But when Father Fox stopped, turned to Bramble and spoke, his voice was surprisingly gentle. "Son, I know you're uncomfortable around Homer, and I understand. But that doesn't change anything. You are lucky to have your family and the safety of your home. Homer can't find his family or his home. If we don't help him, he may be lost for good." HUMAN DIGNITY 3a,b

"Can't God take care of him?" Bramble asked.

"God took care of him by sending him to us. Now he's warm and dry, and your mother's feeding him. If things go well, he'll be back home soon. All you have to do is take him fishing. Imagine how scared he must

be. It will mean a lot to him right now, and it will mean a lot to me."

"Yes sir," Bramble said. He felt bad for the way he was acting, but he couldn't help it. If a skunk sprayed you, you wouldn't be able to hang out with your friends for weeks! Bramble hoped he'd find his parents fast so he could go live in his own home.

Night came and everyone laid down to sleep. The bed was too crowded with Homer in it, and Bramble struggled to get his whole body on the bedding. The den smelled all wrong, too. To make matters worse, Homer had a bad dream in the middle of the night that made him toss and kick, keeping Bramble awake.

His first thought was that Homer would get so afraid in the dream he might spray the whole family with skunk smell in real life! Just when he was about to wake his father and ask him what to do, Bramble heard Homer call out, "Momma! Momma! Where are you, Momma?"

Bramble felt a pang in his chest. He imagined what it would be like to be separated from his family and not know if he'd ever see them again. He remembered how scared he was when he got lost with Tracker chasing

the butterfly. And that was only for a few hours. This little skunk had been away from home for days. And he was all alone!

Bramble shook Homer gently until he woke. He pulled the little skunk closer to him, and felt his whole body trembling. "It's okay, Homer. You were

Bramble shook Homer gently until he woke.

just having a bad dream," Bramble told him. But they both knew the truth. It wasn't just a bad dream. He was really lost. And somewhere out there, his parents were trying to find him.

"Will I ever get home?" Homer asked.

"Sure you will," Bramble answered. But, the truth was, he didn't know.

Bramble lay awake, holding tightly to the skunk until he felt him drift off to sleep. Even then, Bramble refused to sleep. He had to think a way to help. He wouldn't rest until he had.

> *Bramble refused to sleep.*
> *He had to think a way to help.*

At some point in the night, he came up with a plan.

Bramble was the first one out of bed the next morning. He told Father Fox where he was going and took off. Homer and Star were still sleeping when he left.

Bramble was sure his friend Fletch could find Homer's family. Fletch was a hawk, and hawks could cover a lot of ground in a very short time, not to mention their amazing eyesight. And Fletch would

have a lot of hawk friends who could help.

Fletch was up for the challenge. He flew off, promising to get to work right away.

Bramble ran back home. He was determined to keep Homer's mind off things until Fletch returned with news. They would spend the day exploring the Woodlands together.

He was determined to keep Homer's mind off things until Fletch returned with news.

It was nearly time for the evening meal when Bramble and Homer came wandering back to the burrow. Over the course of the day the two had become rather close. Bramble felt awful that Homer might never see his parents again. It no longer mattered to him what his friends thought about him hanging around with a skunk. Being a good friend to Homer was more important.

When the two neared the den, Bramble heard voices inside he didn't recognize. Just before he stepped into the door, he heard Homer shout, "Momma!" then run into the burrow ahead of him.

By the time Bramble caught up with Homer inside the den, he found Homer held tightly between two adult skunks.

"My baby! I thought we'd lost you forever!" one of them cried.

It was Homer's parents!

It was then that Bramble noticed Fletch. Mother and Father Fox and Star were there, too. And they all had tears in their eyes.

Homer's mother and father clung tightly to him, kissing him and stroking his head. Mother Skunk was crying as she spoke to her son.

Bramble was confused by what he saw. "Why is everyone crying?" he asked. "Aren't you all happy?"

"We're all very happy," Mother Fox said. She walked over to Bramble, drying her eyes. "Sometimes, when you're extra happy, you cry. It doesn't mean you're sad. It just means you're filled with emotion." She put her arms around Bramble and squeezed him tight.

Homer's father looked up from the happy reunion. "Thank you so much for all your trouble," he said, looking at each of them. "You have no idea how thankful we are to you for keeping our son safe and

cared for. And you," he said, looking at Fletch, "you spent all day helping Homer, and you didn't even know him. God bless you all."

"It was no trouble," Father Fox said. "In fact, seeing you three together again has made today one of the happiest of our lives."

"It sure has," Bramble said.

And he was happy for Homer. But he also realized he'd probably never see him again. Losing Homer would be sad, but it was okay, because he had learned to care about his friend more than he cared about himself.

And although Homer was leaving, Bramble knew that he would never again judge another animal just because he was different. HUMAN DIGNITY 3b That was something Homer had given Bramble that would never go away.

CHAPTER 21
Tracker's Sour Note

Bramble stood by the bank of Silver Creek shaking himself off. Willow was teaching him how to swim underwater.

It was not going well.

"I hate to admit it," Willow said. "but you may need to stick to dog paddling."

Bramble was about to protest, when he heard something that made the hair on the back of his neck stand on end. "What. Was. That?"

Willow listened. "Either someone is crying out in pain or that's someone singing."

"Someone's in pain, all right," Bramble said. "Me! That singing is awful!" He listened some more. "You know what, Willow? I think I know that voice."

Bramble ran into the woods. There, just through the tree line, was Tracker, perched on a rock, belting out an off-key version of the Happy Birthday song.

Bramble winced. It was the worst thing he'd ever heard.

Tracker noticed Bramble and stopped singing. "Oh Bramble, I didn't know you were there."

Bramble winced. It was the worst thing he'd ever heard.

Bramble eyed his friend closely. What was Tracker doing? "Singing Happy Birthday to yourself, buddy?"

Tracker laughed. "No, silly. It's for my sister. Her birthday is in two days, so I'm practicing. It's going to be my gift to her."

"Does she know?" Bramble asked.

"No," Tracker said. "I want it to be a surprise."

Bramble shook his head. "She'll be surprised, all right."

Tracker looked worried. "What? It's no good? Tell me honestly."

Bramble didn't know what to say. He didn't want to hurt his friend's feelings, so he thought quickly. "It was great, Tracker. I'm sure she'll love it," he said, then forced his mouth into a smile.

He didn't want to hurt his friend's feelings, so he thought quickly.

Later that day, Bramble went to his father. "Is it ever okay to tell a lie?"

"Why do you ask?"

"I heard Tracker practicing Happy Birthday to sing

TRACKER'S SOUR NOTE

to his sister. He asked me if he sounded okay." Bramble looked down. "What could I say?"

"Was it that bad?" Father Fox asked.

"I suppose there are worse ways to die," Bramble joked.

Father Fox chuckled. "I'm sure you meant well." He sighed. "Problem is, there is no such thing as a harmless lie. At the very least, it gets you in the habit of saying what you think folks want to hear. Sooner or later you get caught in one of your lies, and from that moment on folks wonder about everything you say."

What should he have told his friend?

Bramble thought about this. It made sense. But what should he have told his friend?

"Think about it son," Father Fox continued. "God always tells the truth. That must mean honesty is always the right thing to do." TRUTH Ia,b,c

"You mean I should have told Tracker he has an awful voice?"

"Of course not," Father Fox said. "He'll find that out on his own one day. Just remember there are always good things you can say that are true."

"Like what?" Bramble asked.

"Like once I told my dad a joke I'd heard. He didn't laugh, and when I asked him if it was any good, he said I told it very, very well."

"So what should I tell Tracker?"

Father Fox smiled. "Tell him the truth. That Violet is lucky to have a brother who loves her as much as he does."

Bramble smiled. Why hadn't he thought of that! He looked at his father and smiled. "How did you ever learn so many things?"

"Just wait until you have kids of your own. You'll get lots of practice."

The next day Bramble and Tracker met up to play in the meadow. Tracker had some news. He had learned a new song from his mother, and he wanted Bramble's honest opinion.

Bramble clamped his teeth while Tracker struggled through the song. At least he didn't sing any worse than he had the day before!

"Well? What did you think?" Tracker asked when he had finished.

"Well, I . . ."

"Tell me the truth, Bramble. How was it?" Tracker insisted.

Bramble took a deep breath. "Tracker," he said, "your sister is lucky to have a brother who loves her as much as you do."

Tracker laughed. "That's what my dad said. In other words, I can't sing."

Bramble was surprised. Tracker was taking it so well. "You're not upset?" he asked.

"No, not at all! Fact is, I didn't think I sang well until you said I did. I'd much rather give her some pine cones."

"Pine cones?" Bramble asked.

"Yeah. There's this special kind that grows on Crown Hill. Violet loves to use them to decorate our cave. It will take me a few trips to get them, but it will be worth it to make her happy."

"You know what, Tracker," Bramble said. "Your sister really is lucky to have a brother like you."

Tracker smiled. "And I'm lucky to have a friend like you."

CHAPTER 22
Bramble's Bedtime

One of Tracker and Bramble's favorite places was a spot on top of Crown Hill where they could watch the boats go by on the river. From far above, they could see everything from small fishing boats to big ships scurry about the water. One day, while they were taking it all in, Bramble looked up and saw the sun was beginning to set.

"Oh no!" he said. "The sun is touching the tree tops!"

"Relax, Bramble," Tracker said. "It only looks that way. The sun never touches anything on the ground."

Bramble jumped to his feet and shook his head. "No. I mean it's time for me to be home. I'm supposed to be back before the sun sets."

Tracker's mouth hung open in shock. "You mean you've never seen the sun set from the top of Crown Hill? You've never seen the shapes in the stars?"

"Shapes in the stars?" Bramble asked.

"Sure! There are animals and trees and birds and a big path called the Milky Way." Tracker laid back in the grass, looked up at the sky, and smiled. "I like the Big Bear best."

"The big bear?" Bramble asked. "You mean Old Moe?"

"No, silly! This bear is much bigger than Old Moe."

A big bear in the sky, bigger than Old Moe? It all sounded wonderful to Bramble. "You can see all that after the sun sets?"

"Yup!" Tracker said, smiling proudly. "Well, I didn't used to when I was little. But now that I'm older, I get to stay up late, as long as Mom and Dad know where I am."

> *It bothered Bramble that he couldn't stay up late to see the shapes in the stars.*

It bothered Bramble that he couldn't stay up late to see the shapes in the stars. And now Tracker probably thought he was a baby because he had to go home. But what could he do? It was his bedtime soon.

By the time Bramble reached the burrow, the sun had almost completely set. Both Mother and Father Fox were waiting for him.

"Where have you been, Bramble?" his mother asked when she saw him. "We were very worried about you."

Bramble hung his head. "Sorry, mother," he said. "I was on Crown Hill watching the boats with Tracker."

"Well it's a good thing you got home when you did," his father said. "A little longer and you would have been in big trouble."

> *"When you show more responsibility, you will be able to stay up later and go farther on your own."*

Bramble's ears pulled back. He didn't want to be in trouble, but he was missing out on so much! He wasn't a little baby anymore. Why couldn't he have a later bedtime, too? There must be something he could do.

"Tracker said that after the sun sets, you can see shapes in the stars. How come I never get to see them?" Bramble whined.

Father Fox walked over to his son and placed a paw on his shoulder. "You earn more privileges by showing more responsibility. When you show more responsibility, you will be able to stay up later and go farther on your own."

BRAMBLE'S BEDTIME 173

Bramble's ears popped up. Show more responsibility? Surely he could do that! But how? "How can I show more responsibility?" he asked.

Father Fox smiled. "What do you think?"

Bramble thought a moment. What kinds of things would he need to do in order to show responsibility? "Hmmm," Bramble said. "Show you I'm smart enough not to get lost?"

"That's important, but that's not it," Father Fox said.

Bramble tried again. "Prove I'm fast enough to run away from danger?"

Father Fox shook his head. "That certainly helps, but that's not it either."

"I know! Be strong enough to win in a fight! Grrrr!" Bramble said, then bounced around Father Fox boxing the air.

Father Fox laughed and ruffled the top of Bramble's head. "Being strong is important, but that's not what I'm looking for."

Bramble thought as hard as he could. "I don't know!" he said. "What is it?"

"You keep thinking about it, then tell me what you

come up with," Father Fox said.

Bramble sat and thought as hard as he could but couldn't imagine what else it could be. He became very frustrated. About that time, Mother Fox called out to Star.

"Star, honey. Have you finished your chores? It's almost time for bed," she said.

"Yes, Mother," Star said. "Do you want to check?"

"No, dear," her mother said. "I don't need to. If you say you've done them, I know I can trust you."

Bramble's ears shot up, and he jumped to his feet. That was it! Trust!

"I know what it is, Father!" he said, bouncing on his hind legs. "It's trust! I can stay up later when I can be trusted to do what I'm told! Is that it?" he asked.

Father Fox smiled. "It is about trust," he said, "but it's not about me trusting you to do what you're told. I'll know you're responsible when you don't have to be told what to do. When you make right choices on your own, even when no one is watching."

"You mean like the time Tracker and I cleaned up Mister Beaver's pond?" he asked.

"I'll tell you the stories about the shapes in the stars."

176 FRIENDS OF THE WOODLANDS TRAIL

"Yes," Father Fox said. "That's a good example."

"And the time I learned sign language so Buck wouldn't feel alone?"

"Yes, that's exactly what I mean." Father Fox smiled, but then his face turned serious, and he was quiet. After a moment, he placed a paw under Bramble's chin. "You know what, son? I think you are ready for a little more freedom."

"You know what, son? I think you are ready for a little more freedom."

"Really?" Bramble said jumping about. He stopped and hugged his father tightly.

"I tell you what, son," Father Fox said. "Let's go up on top of Crown Hill together and check out the stars. Just the two of us."

Bramble's eyes widened. "Tonight?"

"Yes, sir! Tonight. And if we hurry, we can catch the sun set. After that, I'll tell you the stories about the shapes in the stars."

"Yipee!" Bramble cheered.

"And while we're there," his father continued, "we

can talk a little more about growing up. And maybe we can do something about that bedtime of yours."

Bramble could hardly contain himself. Not only was he getting to stay up later, he knew he had earned his father's trust. More than anything else, making his father proud made him feel all grown up.

CHAPTER 23
Mister Ranger's Flag

Tracker was not a morning animal. He didn't do early. So when Bramble asked him if he would join him to watch the sunrise on Crown Hill the next day, he almost said no. But Bramble insisted, and he eventually gave in.

When Bramble showed up at the cave that morning, Tracker wanted to

"We have to go watch Mister Ranger."

tell his friend he'd changed his mind. But Bramble promised that once they started walking, he would feel better.

Bramble was wrong. Tracker still missed his bed as they trudged up Crown Hill. When he finally saw the red circle of the sun rising, he was less than impressed.

"It's just like the sunset only backward," Tracker said. He yawned. "I'm going back to bed."

"Not yet," Bramble said. "We have to go watch

Mister Ranger."

"What are you talking about?" Tracker asked.

"Every morning, just after sunrise, I see him do the most interesting thing. Let's go ask him about it."

Tracker decided to go with Bramble, but he warned him that it better be worth keeping him out of bed for.

"Every morning, just after sunrise, I see him do the most interesting thing."

When they arrived at the cabin, Mister Ranger was just stepping out into the yard. He carried a folded cloth under his arm, and was making his way to the flagpole. Tracker and Bramble ran to meet him.

"Good morning, Mister Ranger. What are you doing?" Tracker asked.

"Good morning, fellas," he said. "I'm raising my flag."

Tracker watched as he carefully unfolded the cloth. It had holes on one end, which he clipped to the flagpole's rope. Tracker was intrigued. "Is that your flag?" he asked.

"It is," Mister Ranger told him. "I have to be careful

"Is that your flag?" he asked.

MISTER RANGER'S FLAG 181

not to let it touch the ground."

"Why?" Tracker asked. "Will it get dirty?"

"No. Because it's one of our country's symbols."

"What's a country?" Bramble asked.

Mister Ranger pulled the rope. As he did, the flag moved slowly up the flagpole. "A country is a place where people live together and work together," he continued.

"Like the Woodlands?" Tracker asked.

"Yes, sort of like the Woodlands," he said. "Only much bigger. All the people who live in our country have made a promise to follow a set of rules. These rules make people feel safe and let them know they will be treated fairly." TRUTH 1a,b

"Aaaaah," Tracker said. But he still didn't understand.

Mister Ranger went on. "Our country is called America, and our set of rules is called the Constitution. Both our country and our constitution have been around for a very long time."

"Since before I was born?" Bramble asked.

"Since before even my parents and grandparents

were born," he said. "These rules are a lot like the rules on the front gate of the campsite. They're there to help protect the things we all love so they'll be around long after we're gone."

"Oooooh," Tracker said. It was beginning to make sense.

"But our country's constitution doesn't just protect things we can see and touch like the trees and the creek. It also protects ideas like honesty, loyalty, and freedom. You might not understand these ideas yet, but you enjoy them every day."

The flag reached the top of the pole, and Mister Ranger ... took a step back and saluted the flag.

The flag reached the top of the pole, and Mister Ranger tied the rope at the bottom. He took a step back and saluted the flag.

"So that's a country," Tracker said. "But what's a symbol?"

Mister Ranger smiled. "Think of the flag as a picture of something. You've seen the picture of the mountains in my cabin, right? That's a picture of something

you can see. The flag is a picture of something you can't see. Something you can only feel inside. That's what makes it a symbol."

"Oh, I see," Tracker said, scratching his ear. "At least I think I do. But how do you know what a feeling's symbol should look like?"

"You can never be sure, but the flag is the best symbol of our country that has ever been made."

"It is?" Bramble asked. "How so?"

"Well, just take a look."

Bramble and Tracker looked up at the colorful flag, stretched out in the wind.

"The blue square stands for truth," Mister Ranger told them. "Not just for things that are so, but for the importance of keeping your promises and being honest and fair."

"I see," Tracker said. "What else?"

"Well, the white means purity; that means all the love and goodness in you that makes your thoughts, words, and deeds pleasing to God."

"What about the red part?" Bramble said. "It's like my fur."

Mister Ranger laughed. "Yes, it is, but that's not what it stands for. The red is a picture of courage. Truth and purity are fine things, but, to make them count, you must also be brave. These red stripes remind

> "It should never be allowed to touch the ground. That's one way we show respect."

you to do what is right, even when it's hard and you feel frightened. There were many great people who worked very hard, kept their promises, and showed a lot of courage to take care of our country."

TRUTH Ic

"There were?" Tracker asked. "They did all that for our country?

"They sure did. They saw this flag and it reminded them of all the important things our country was designed for. Some of them even died so that others might live."

"Wow," Tracker said. "That is a good picture."

"Yes, it's a very good picture. And it should never be allowed to touch the ground. That's one way we

show respect. Not just for the symbol, but for all the people who worked hard and had courage."

"Are there other pictures of things you can only feel?" Bramble asked.

"Yes," Mister Ranger said, reaching inside his shirt and pulling out a thin gold chain with a small cross. He showed it to the boys. "This is another picture of truth, purity, and courage. But this one is even better, because it's also a picture of love." CREATION 2b,c

Tracker looked at the cross thoughtfully. "Did anyone ever die for it?"

Mister Ranger smiled. "That is a very important question, Tracker. And I'd love to tell you about it."

Tracker couldn't wait. He could tell it was going to be a good story. He smiled at Bramble. "Thanks for making me come out here, Bramble. I guess there are a few things worth waking up early for."

CHAPTER 24
The First Snow

After the first snow had fallen and Beaver Pond had frozen over, the otters began ice skating across the pond's smooth surface. While the otters skated, Tracker and Bramble played on the shoreline, rolling snow into giant balls that they could use to make a snowman.

Bramble was working hard but Tracker kept getting distracted.

Bramble was working hard, but Tracker kept getting distracted. He stared at the otters gliding across the ice. A few were speed skating across the pond. Others were spinning in circles.

Bramble frowned when he noticed that Tracker wasn't helping build the snowman. "Hey, whatcha lookin' at?"

Tracker sighed. "Oh just the otters. Ice skating looks like fun! I wish we could join them. I'd be a great

ice skater!"

Bramble turned and watched the otters playing on the ice. "Yeah, but remember what your dad and my dad said? Only otters can play on the ice. We're too big. If the ice broke, we'd fall through and get hurt."

Tracker crossed his arms. He didn't think it was fair. Then an idea popped into his mind. "Maybe I'll come back later when everyone's gone and give this ice skating thing a try. I'm not that big. It'll probably be fine. Even if I get a little wet, who cares?"

Tracker knelt down and packed some snow into a tight ball. Then he flung the snowball at Bramble and darted away.

The snowball hit Bramble on the shoulder. "Hey!" Bramble shouted. "I wasn't ready!" He grabbed some snow off the snowman and raced after Tracker. "Come back! I've got a present for you!"

For the next ten minutes, Tracker and Bramble chased each other and threw dozens of snowballs. When at last they'd worn themselves out, they sat on an old log to rest.

"That sure was fun!" Bramble said, trying to catch his breath. He looked up at the sun that was far off on

one side of the sky. "Well, I'd better get going. I've got chores to do before it gets dark."

Tracker waved goodbye to his buddy. He watched Bramble disappear into the forest. As the minutes passed, Tracker saw the otters waddle away to their dens. The sky was starting to grow dim as the sun began to drop behind the mountain.

"Now's my chance!" Tracker thought. The only otter still ice skating was Willow. Tracker scurried to the edge of the pond and waved his arms, trying to catch Willow's attention.

"That sure looks like fun! Is it hard to ice skate?"

It didn't take long for Willow to notice Tracker. He glided effortlessly over to the young lion.

Tracker's face lit up. "That sure looks like fun! Is it hard to ice skate?"

"Not at all," Willow answered. "It's easy."

"Can you teach me?"

Willow scratched his head in confusion. "Are you allowed to go on the ice? I thought you're not supposed to."

"Of course it's fine," Tracker said. "I just need a few tips on how to skate. That's why I waited around to ask you. You're obviously the best skater!"

A huge grin spread across Willow's face. "That's right! I've been practicing for several years." Willow rubbed his chin for a moment. "Fine, I'll show you how to ice skate, but make sure to stay near the edge of the pond." Willow pointed to the middle of the pond. "Whatever you do, stay away from the center. The ice is thinner out there."

"Okay, I got it."

"Then follow me!" Willow said. He turned and skated out over the ice.

Tracker tried to follow him, but when his paws hit the ice, they slid out from under him.

Tracker tried to follow him, but when his paws hit the ice, they slid out from under him, and he crashed down onto his belly. "Ouch!" he yelled.

Willow chuckled, then said, "You have to start gently. Slowly. Like this." The otter moved over the ice with confidence, gliding

back and forth in front of his friend. When he returned to Tracker, he said, "I have an idea. Why don't you start on the hill? Get a good running start and just let things slide."

Tracker watched as Willow showed him what to do. He made sliding across the ice look like the easiest thing in the world.

Tracker couldn't wait. "Let me at it!" He pounced up the hill. When he reached the top, he turned and faced the pond. His eyes narrowed. "Look out, Willow," he called. "Here I come!" Tracker ran down the hill and leapt onto the ice. He slid fast on his belly, farther than any of the otters had gone. Once he came to a stop, he stood, then slowly turned back toward the hill. "That was amazing!"

He slid fast on his belly, farther than any of the otters had gone.

Tracker couldn't wait to do it again. But as soon as he tried to walk, his paws lost grip and his body came crashing down. "Willow?" he cried, still lying flat on

the ice. "Help me."

Willow laughed, then skated over and helped Tracker walk back toward the hill. "Wow, you sure did go far! Maybe the hill isn't such a good idea. You might go too far and fall through the center."

Tracker shook his head. "No, I'm fine. Now that I skated once, I know what I'm doing."

Willow's whiskers twitched. "It takes lots of practice to become a good skater. I have to get going, but we could practice again tomorrow."

"You really shouldn't play on the ice alone," Willow said. "It's not safe."

Tracker gave Willow a pat on the back. "Sounds good. I'm just gonna practice a little bit more."

"You really shouldn't play on the ice alone," Willow said. "It's not safe."

Tracker huffed. "Don't worry. I'll be careful."

"All right," Willow said. "If you say so. But if you were really being careful, you'd go home."

Willow said goodbye, then left.

Tracker snickered. He wasn't a scaredy-cat. Now that he had the whole pond to himself, he could practice until he was an expert skater.

Tracker climbed to the top of the hill, then turned and faced the ice. His ears went back, his eyes narrowed. His tail thrashed back and forth. This would be his best slide yet!

When he reached the edge of the ice, he leapt forward and dove onto his belly, his legs spread out on either side.

Tracker sprung off his hind legs and ran as fast as he could down the hill. When he reached the edge of the ice, he leapt forward and dove onto his belly, his legs spread out on either side. As he slid across the surface, he lost control and started spinning. He kept sliding and spinning, unable to stop.

Then, before he knew it, he realized he was headed straight for the middle of the pond—straight for the thin ice!

As he neared the middle, he began to slow. When he finally came to a stop, he took a deep breath. *Whoa, that was close!* He began standing on his legs,

but stopped when he heard a deep crackling sound. Tiny cracks splintered through the ice all around him.

Tracker knew he was in danger. He had to get off the thin ice as fast as he could. He took a quick breath then jumped toward the shore. But because the ice was so slippery, he didn't jump more than a few feet. When he landed on the ice, his paws slipped out from beneath him and he crashed onto his side.

The ice instantly crumbled into a hundred pieces. Before he knew what had happened, Tracker plunged into the coldest water he'd ever felt.

The shock of the freezing water took his breath away. It was so cold, it hurt! Tracker tried to climb out. He clawed at the ice, but all he did was scratch the slick surface. The more he fought to get out, the more pieces of ice broke off and crowded the water around him.

Tracker panicked. "Help me! Somebody, HELP!"

Tracker shouted as loud as he could. He yelled again and again, but he didn't see anyone on shore. If only he'd listened to Willow. Being alone on the ice was dangerous. He wasn't supposed to be on the ice at all! What had he been thinking?

The cold quickly zapped Tracker's energy. He fought hard to stay above the icy surface, but the cold made it hard to breathe.

Then, out of nowhere, Tracker felt a strong hand reach out and grab him tightly. He felt himself being pulled back onto the ice and dragged toward shore. Tracker gulped in huge breaths of air. Then, suddenly, everything around him went dark and still.

When Tracker opened his eyes, he was wrapped in a blanket by Mister Ranger's fireplace hearth, the warmth of the fire soaked through his fur and warmed him to the bone. He looked around. Mister Ranger, Mother and Father Lion, and even his sister Violet were all in the room.

Suddenly, everything around him went dark and still.

Violet saw him him looking around. "Look!" she said. "He's awake!"

Tracker tried to sit up, but was too weak to lift his shoulders.

"You just rest there, little fellow," Mister Ranger said.

Mother Lion rushed over to her son with Father Lion close behind. "Thank God you're alright," his mom said.

Father Lion's face was full of worry. "You gave us quite a scare!"

Tracker tried to smile, but felt weak. He glanced over at Mister Ranger. "You saved my life.

Mister Ranger shrugged. "It wasn't me," he said. "I heard a knock at the door and, when I answered it, you were lying there on my front porch—wet, cold, and completely unconscious. I don't know who brought you here, but whoever it was, that person is the hero."

Mother Lion stroked the fur on top of Tracker's head. "You don't have any idea who brought him here?"

Mister Ranger shook his head. "No idea. My guess is that several animals must have been nearby. When they heard him splashing around, they rescued him. But I don't know why they wouldn't want to take credit for helping him."

Father Lion took a deep breath. "I'm so thankful someone was around to rescue Tracker. But in addition to those animals, the Lord was also providing help. I'm

reminded of Psalm 46:l. That verse says, 'God is our refuge and strength, a very present help in trouble.'"

PROVIDENCE 6a,b,c

Tracker tried to think back to what had happened. He remembered the fear he felt, thinking that he might drown or freeze to death. He remembered thinking he would never see his family again. And then he remem-

Tracker rememebr thinking he would never see his family again .

THE FIRST SNOW

bered that strong hand pulling him out of the water and dragging him to safety.

Mister Ranger reached over to the wood stack and placed another dry branch in the fireplace. "Well, God certainly is watching over Tracker." He glanced at the young lion. "I'm so glad you're okay."

"Absolutely!" Mother Lion said. She reached down and gave Tracker a huge hug.

Father Lion nodded. The worry in his face began to melt away.

Tracker still felt weak. He also had an awful headache, but he was glad to be alive. He closed his eyes and said a quick prayer. "Thank you, God, for sending someone to rescue me!"

Tracker knew he had done wrong by sliding out on the ice. That was a mistake—a terrible mistake that he would never do again. From now on, he would listen to his parents' rules and warnings. And he would live knowing that every day is a gift from God.

CHAPTER 25
A Christmas Story

It was nearly sunset. Mother Fox was giving Bramble and Star a bath just outside the den. Bramble and Star hated bathtime.

"Hold still and stop squirming," Mother Fox said to Bramble. "The better you sit still, the sooner this will be over."

"Why do you give us a bath every day?" Star asked. "We'll only get dirty again."

Mother Fox smiled and tapped her on the nose. "Why do you get dirty every day? You'll only get another bath," she said, then went back to cleaning behind Bramble's ears.

Just then, Fletch landed beside them. "Big news! You won't believe it."

"What is it?" Bramble asked.

"So I was flying last night to get a better look at the full moon when I saw these spectacular colored lights

below me."

"Really? What were they?" Star asked.

"It was wonderful. I flew down close to them, and you'll never guess what I saw."

"What? What?" Bramble asked, impatiently. Fletch always did like to draw his stories out for effect.

"Mister Ranger has put thousands of little lights all over the bushes outside his cabin. I mean they're everywhere! It was just like a city looks at night from above. It was beautiful!"

"Let's go see!" Bramble said.

"Yeah!" shouted Star.

"Mister Ranger has put thousands of little lights all over the bushes outside his cabin."

"Uh, uh, uh," Mother Fox said. "Not until you've both had your baths. I won't have you visiting Mister Ranger in this condition."

"Aww, man!" Bramble said.

Mother Fox stopped bathing and looked at Bramble sternly. "Watch your tone, young man, or you won't be going at all."

Bramble cringed. "Oops. Sorry, mother. I meant, yes, ma'am."

"That's better."

Fletch waited for Bramble and Star to have their baths. Once they were finished, the three of them went to get Tracker so he could come, too.

Tracker found the whole thing confusing. "Why would Mister Ranger put lights on bushes? It doesn't make sense."

"Well let's go ask him," Bramble said. "Fletch said it's like flying over a city, whatever that means."

Fletch laughed. "Oh, yeah. I guess that wouldn't make sense to you. Let's just say it's sparkly and bright, kind of like the stars at night."

"Stars in the bushes?" Tracker said. "This I've gotta' see."

So the four of them set off for Mister Ranger's.

When they arrived, Mister Ranger was hanging a circle of leaves on his front door.

Star ran ahead of the others when she saw him. "Hiya, Mister Ranger! Whatcha' doin'?"

Mister Ranger turned and smiled. "Good evening,

Star," he said. "Good evening, boys. To what do I owe this pleasure?"

"Why do you put lights on the bushes?" Tracker asked.

Mister Ranger laughed deeply. "Well, Tracker. Those are called Christmas lights. And now that the sun is setting, I'll be turning them on soon. Do you kids want to help me?"

"Oh, boy! Yippee!" Star said, hopping from foot to foot.

> *"The wreath and the lights are both symbols of Christmas."*

"But why are you putting those leaves on your door?" Fletch asked.

"Well, Fletch, that's called a wreath. The wreath and the lights are both symbols of Christmas."

"Symbols?" Bramble asked. "Like the flag?" he said, looking back at the flagpole.

"That's exactly right, Bramble." Mister Ranger paused for a moment and looked toward the cabin, then turned back to them. "Why don't you four come inside for a bit. I want to show you something."

The first thing Bramble saw when they got inside was that Mister Ranger had a pine tree in a corner of the living room. It was covered with many shiny and

"Wow!" Star said, her face glowing. "It's so pretty!"

colorful things of all different shapes and sizes. When he looked to the top, he saw a shining star had been placed there.

"Wow!" Star said, her face glowing. "It's so pretty!"

"Wow is right," Fletch said.

Tracker walked up close to the tree and carefully touched some of the stringy, shiny things that were laid over each branch. "Where did you find a tree like this," he asked.

"It was just a regular tree until I decorated it," Mister Ranger said. "Wait, I saved the best for last." He bent behind the tree and pressed a long snake-like thing into the wall. When he did, the tree lit up like the night sky.

"But what is Christmas?" Bramble asked.

"Wooooow!" the four friends said together, their heads leaned back, their eyes wide.

"Now that's what I call a tree!" Bramble said. "But why did you do it?"

Mister Ranger folded his arms in front of him. "Well, kids," he began. "It's almost Christmas."

"But what is Christmas?" Bramble asked.

"Well, I'll tell you," Mister Ranger began. "You see, long ago, when the world had lost its way, it needed a very special gift from God. So God sent a baby." CREATION 2a,b,c

He knelt by the tree and picked up a small group of figurines standing on a platform, then passed it around for each of them to hold. "See the baby?" he asked. "Just like foxes and mountain lions and hawks start out small and helpless, the baby God sent—like the one you see in this manger—was very tiny. His mother named him Jesus and wrapped Him up in a blanket to keep Him warm."

"Did he grow up to be a ranger like you? With rules for people to follow?" Star asked.

"In a way, I suppose. Only His rules were even better than mine."

Fletch handed the manger scene back to Mister Ranger. "I'm not sure I like rules." TRUTH Ia,b,c

"But rules are important, Fletch," Tracker said "Without rules for the campers, we wouldn't be able to enjoy the forest like we do."

"That's right, Tracker."

A CHRISTMAS STORY 205

"So what were His rules?" Bramble asked.

Mister Ranger smiled. "He said 'Love one another as I have loved you.'"

"Oh," Fletch said. "I like that rule. But what does it all have to do with Christmas?"

"Good question," Mister Ranger said. "You see, when this baby was born, there was a special star in the sky—we'll call it the Christmas Star—and it told everyone the good news. That's why I have a star on top of my tree."

> *"When this baby was born, there was a special star in the sky—we'll call it the Christmas Star—and it told everyone the good news."*

"Oooooh," the four friends said in unison, looking again at the star on top of the tree.

"Important people travelled a long way to see this baby, and they brought him gifts. Since that time, it has been our custom to give gifts to the ones we love at Christmas. That's the day we remember the birth of Jesus."

"That makes sense," Brambles said, nodding.

"Christmas is a special time of love and joy. I love

you all every day of the year, but Christmas is a very special time of profound love, to remember when God gave us the greatest gift of all. Now why don't you all come over here and sit in front of the fire. I have gifts for you. After that, we can go outside, and you can all help me turn on the lights."

Mister Ranger brought them in front of the fire and gave each of them a sweet treat.

"We love our gifts, Mister Ranger, but we have nothing to give you," Bramble said, his mouth full of chocolate.

Mister Ranger sat down next to them and smiled. "The best gift you can give me is yourself," he said, then opened his arms for a big hug.

"Did I just give you a gift, or was that another gift from you?" Star asked.

Mister Ranger laughed. "Well, Star, love is special that way. It feels good both giving and receiving it. And love is what Christmas is all about."

208   FRIENDS OF THE WOODLANDS TRAIL

SAY HELLO TO
The Woodlands Pals Team

John Burkitt, author of the Premier Edition of *The Trailman's Handbook for Navigators and Adventurers* and contributor to countless other projects, brings his story-telling to the Woodlands Pals. We are thankful for his commitment to youth and to delivering the virtues and character-building morals that make it fun for boys to learn to Walk Worthy!

Leigh Elizabeth, mother to four Trailmen, brings the Woodlands Pals to life through her expressive illustrations. Don't tell her boys, but we think there is more than a slight resemblance to the Pals!

Jessica R. Everson edited these stories. She is the mother of nine-year-old hiking enthusiast Vonché. We are thankful to Jessica for turning the written word visual, and to Vonché for his approval of these messages.

Anna Jelstrom displayed her excellence in design and layout here, as she has with every major published Trail Life USA book. But she says this book was the most fun!

FORWARD FOR PARENTS

Welcome to the Woodlands Trail, the beginning of an adventure for your son that starts in the Woodlands and leads him to the Timberline before he becomes a Navigator. Along the way he'll encounter challenges, new experiences, opportunities to grow, and great friendships.

With his Trail Life Troop he'll enjoy outdoor adventure, character growth, leadership opportunity, and Christian fellowship in a robust yet flexible program built on the enduring foundation of God's Word.

This program was developed with four goals: First, it values personal growth over recognitions. Second, it creates a sense of belonging and familiarity among all Woodlands Trail age groups so that a young boy joining the program as a five-year old will be exposed to the concepts that he will encounter in the Navigators and Adventurers programs ahead. Third, it allows younger boys to benefit from the experience of older youth while giving more mature boys a chance to become mentors. Finally, it is easy to administer under a variety of circumstances.

It is our hope that the fun and challenge of the Woodlands Trail will encourage boys to follow the Trail Life all the way into manhood, and that each boy will be strengthened spiritually as well as physically and mentally.

If you regularly attend with your child, you may want to consider the Registered Adult position. The Registered Adult position is for registering parents or guardians who, while not serving in an official leadership position, may want to have a more active role with their boys in the program.

V

CONTENTS

Levels of Troop Support for Families   viii

SECTION 1
the trail life story of the trail   1

SECTION 2
what are the basics?   9

The Basics of the Woodlands Trail Program   9

Requirements for Membership in Trail Life USA   9

Specific Requirements for Youth Membership   11

What about Safety?   12

Wisdom for Using Technology   14

Tread Lightly!® Principles   18

Christian Worldview Principles   20

SECTION 3
how does the program work?   22

Learning in the Woodlands Trail Program   22

Woodlands Trail Awards Overview   24

Branch Awards and Branch Pins   24

Forest Awards and Sylvan Stars   27

Special Awards   28

Summer Months   31

Trailmen with Special Needs   31

SECTION 4
where does my son start?   32

How to Earn the Branch Patch Joining Award   32

SECTION 5

what do trailmen wear?   38

The Trail Life USA Uniform	38
Uniform and Insignia Guide	40

SECTION 6

how does a trailman advance in his troop?   41

Summary of Steps: Core Steps and Elective Steps	41
'Hit the Trail!' Activities	42
Family Home Activities	42
Requirements per Level	43
Requirements for Heritage Branch `tab`	45
Requirements for Hobbies Branch `tab`	54
Requirements for Life Skills Branch `tab`	61
Requirements for Outdoor Skills Branch `tab`	72
Requirements for Science and Technology Branch `tab`	83
Requirements for Sports and Fitness Branch `tab`	92
Requirements for Values Branch `tab`	101

SECTION 7

how do we track advancements?   112

Fox Patrol Charts	113
Hawk Patrol Charts	119
Mountain Lion Patrol Charts	125

A TRAIL LIFE USA WOODLANDS TRAIL FAMILY'S PERSONAL LEVELS OF TROOP SUPPORT

Where does a family turn to get answers to questions about the program? Here's a good strategy for any Woodlands Trail family to use:

1. **Yourself** – We can read all materials provided and emails or other communications
2. **Online** – We can refer to Trail Life Connect for additional information
3. **Our Troop's Onboarding Facilitator**
4. **Our Troop's Trail Guide(s)**
5. **Our Troop's Woodlands Trail Ranger**
6. **Our Troop's Troopmaster**
7. **Our Troop's Troop Ministry Liaison (TML)**
8. **Other Troop Support (as needed):**
   a. **Committee Chair**
   b. **Troop Treasurer**
   c. **Chaplain**

....

Trail Life is volunteer driven. It is one of our core values!

This means you can take an active role in making your Troop function best, providing your son with the greatest opportunity to benefit from Trail Life.

There are many ways you can help, from occasionally bringing a snack to organizing field trips to full-on Troop level leadership. Some require registration, some don't. Talk with or contact your Troop leadership for more information about ways you can make a difference. If you regularly attend with your child, you may want to consider the Registered Adult position.

The Registered Adult position is for registering parents or guardians who, while not serving in an official leadership position, may want to have a more active role with their boys in the program.

MY TROOP CONTACTS

Our Troop's Troopmaster:

Name _____ Phone _____

Email _____

Our Troop's Woodlands Trail Ranger:

Name _____ Phone _____

Email _____

Our Troop's Trail Guides:

Name _____ Phone _____

Email _____

Name _____ Phone _____

Email _____

Name _____ Phone _____

Email _____

Our Troop's Onboarding Chair:

Name _____ Phone _____

Email _____

Others:

Name _____ Phone _____

Email _____

WALK WORTHY!

"... that you may walk worthy of the Lord, fully pleasing Him, being fruitful in every good work and increasing in the knowledge of God ..."

Colossians 1:10, NKJV

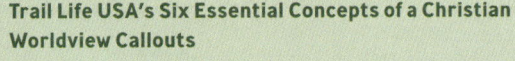

Trail Life USA's Six Essential Concepts of a Christian Worldview Callouts

Trail Life's first Core Value is "Christ-Centered," so we create content that consistently points out biblical truths that will help you to develop a strong Christian Worldview, which is important in guiding you to *Walk Worthy*.

The Trail Life USA Board of Directors has provided Six Essential Concepts of a Christian Worldview. These concepts are identified with a special callout icon throughout this Handbook. The in-line text note identifies which Christian Worldview Essential(s) and subpoints are being referenced. (These can be found on *page 20*.) As you work on advancements and activities, these concepts deserve your attention. You will grow to see more and more how God has built these concepts into all of His creation. Wouldn't it be great if every Trailman became familiar with these concepts, strengthening our own Christian Worldview and our shared values?

---

the trail life
story of the trail

Welcome to the Woodlands Trail!

It's always helpful to know a bit about the trail you are on before you begin.

One of the most meaningful aspects of Trail Life USA is the symbolism built into various parts of the program. Many of these symbols have both a natural and spiritual meaning. Collectively the program levels, patrol levels, Ranks, and Awards tell a story that parallels the central analogy of the program, namely that we are all walking along the trail of life and what Jesus called the "narrow path."

THE TRAILHEAD: THE WOODLANDS TRAIL

A Trailman's adventure begins as most hiking trails do, in the lush, green woods. Trailmen travel on the well-beaten Woodlands Trail, surrounded and protected by the mature, strong trees which stand as sentinels that have watched and guided many young Trailmen along the same trail. In the woodlands, creatures explore the branches during the day and are guided by the light of the stars at night. Woodlands Trailmen earn the Branch Patch and Branch Pins during their first year in a Woodlands Trail patrol. These signify their exploration of skills and topics along seven distinct Branches. As they fill their Branch Patch, they are successfully navigating through the forest of

their first year in a Woodlands Trail patrol on their way toward the Forest Award. After earning the Forest Award, Trailmen will earn Sylvan Star Pins. *Sylvan* is Latin for forest, and the Sylvan Stars in Trail Life symbolize the further exploration of the Woodlands activities that will guide the Trailmen through the dark.

The youngest patrol a Trailman will join in the Woodlands Trail is the **Fox patrol**. In nature, foxes are small, energetic animals found playing and chasing other woodland creatures among the brambles and through the undergrowth. Fox Trailmen are similarly small and energetic. Their activities should be filled with active, fun games and hands-on activities that fit perfectly with their curious nature.

As Trailmen continue along the Woodlands Trail, they enter the **Hawk patrol**. Hawks are observant creatures that can be seen soaring, swooping, and screeching through the trees in the woodlands. Hawk Trailmen have grown in their stature and their adventurous spirit. Their experience in Trail Life will call them to "leave the ground" and go "higher" as they continue to explore the Woodlands Trail Branches.

A Trailman's last patrol on the Woodlands Trail is the **Mountain Lion patrol**. Mountain lions are strong, smart animals that reign among the other woodlands creatures. They can be found everywhere, lurking on the forest floor, reclining high in the branches, or exploring the open boulderland above the timberline. Mountain Lion Trailmen are the oldest Trailmen along the

Timberline Award

2 WOODLANDS TRAIL HANDBOOK

Woodlands Trail, and they alone have the opportunity to earn the capstone award for the Woodlands Trail, the Timberline Award.

The **Timberline Award** symbolizes the Mountain Lion Trailman's completion of the Woodlands Trail program and his additional work of deepening his faith. He has honed his skills and is ready to launch out of the green Woodlands Trail, up past the timberline, and begin navigating the open gray rocky ridges of a new frontier.

ABOVE THE TIMBERLINE: NAVIGATORS AND ADVENTURERS

Above the timberline, Trailmen begin achieving "ranks" in both the Navigator and Adventurer programs. The Navigators program is designed for II-I3-year-old Trailmen and represents the frontier experienced above the timberline, where one leaves the woodlands and begins to trek across open rocky lands of adolescence.

The Navigators program color is gray, representing this new frontier and the new obstacles that the Trailmen will have to overcome. On a hiking trail, when the trail crosses open territory, it can sometimes be easy to lose the trail. One way that hikers know they are on the correct trail is by following trail markers. In Trail Life, Navigator Trailmen will begin to work on Trail Badges that are symbolically their trail markers keeping them on the correct trail toward the peaks. As they continue along the trail, they will earn different rank patches, each with their own unique symbolism.

As a hiker approaches higher elevations, he notices a dramatic shift in the scenery and colors that he encounters. Now he is looking out

THE TRAIL LIFE STORY OF THE TRAIL 3

over the woodlands and the rocky boulder fields he just navigated. As he looks ahead, he sees the blue sky above him, the sun shining, and the mountain peaks.

The Adventurers program is identified by this blue color and the visible peaks and is designed for a 14-17-year-old Trailman who takes full ownership of his adventures, leading himself and other Trailmen along the trail. The Adventurer Trailman will continue up the trail earning Trail Badges and new ranks, all while experiencing new and unique high adventures that will test, stretch, and grow him into a godly man. The Adventurer Trailmen take the lead and set the pace for the patrols and programs behind them.

In the Navigators program, or for Trailmen who join at the Adventurers program level, the first rank earned is the **Recruit Trailman.** The term "recruit" signifies that the Trailman is joining a group of like-minded young men who are all working toward the same goal. He is shown on the patch "reporting for duty." The rank also implies there are other members to follow. The Recruit Trailman begins implementing the Patrol Method—working, studying, and serving in a small group called a patrol. The Recruit Trailman learns from his fellow Trailmen and mentors as he learns how to navigate this new frontier.

The next rank is the **Able Trailman**. The imagery on the rank patch shows a Trailman equipped with the gear he needs, confidently navigating his way across the rocky terrain. His Trailman's Standard displays his earned Trail Badges and reminds him of the lessons he has already learned and inspires him to continue up the trail. The Able Trailman is truly able to navigate his surroundings either by the

Ridgeline Award

knowledge and experience he has gained or by knowing where and how to acquire the needed knowledge and skills.

The third rank is the **Ready Trailman.** The rank patch shows an older man standing strong and steady as he points and leads younger men up the trail. A Ready Trailman knows that both men on the patch represent him. As an older Trailman he stands strong in his knowledge and skills and guides new recruits up the trail. At the same time, the younger man on the patch represents him as he follows the only true guide, Jesus Christ, up the trail towards true freedom. If a Trailman is a Navigator and has earned the Ready Trailman rank, he will have the opportunity to earn the capstone award for the Navigators program, the **Ridgeline Award**. In hiking, the ridgeline is where the terrain becomes steeper and more precarious as hikers prepare to "take the summit." Hikers that traverse the ridgeline are prepared and determined to work through the difficult terrain ahead and finish the trail knowing the exciting adventures that await them on the approach to the summit.

The highest three ranks in Trail Life are reserved for Adventurers only, earning Trail Badges known as **"True Freedom"** badges. As Trailmen traverse up and across the ridgeline, they experience an extraordinary journey as they scramble over talus and move toward the True Freedom found at the summit. The first True Freedom rank is the **Journey Rank**, and its image displays a compass that a Trailman uses to navigate the paths of his journey. The compass guides and gives direction and helps him to avoid taking the wrong trail, becoming lost, or encountering serious danger. Dating back to the time of Aristotle we find references to the concept of virtues being a moral map or compass

THE TRAIL LIFE STORY OF THE TRAIL 5

to guide us in making decisions in life. For the Trailman, the moral compass is the scripture, his conscience, and the wisdom of other believers around him, which can guide him through the journey of life.

The next True Freedom rank is the **Ascent Rank**. After traveling on the journey, the trail often begins to ascend upwards and becomes more difficult and challenging. A Trailman discovers that leadership involves serving others and working together. An older Adventurer Trailman learns to lead younger Navigators and Woodlands Trailmen, helping them up and over the rugged terrain. The firm grip of a Trailman's handshake and the Standard stabilize the older Trailman as he helps the younger Trailman.

The **Horizon Rank** is the highest True Freedom rank. After a long and challenging ascent of learning and leading, the Trailman approaches the peak of this adventure. Just as the hiker nearing the top of the mountain can look out at the vast horizon in all directions, a Horizon Trailman looks out at the new adventures that await him on his horizons. The Horizon Rank features a lit torch that symbolizes how the Trailman will be guided by the true light of Christ, and will let his "light shine before others, so that they may see your good works and give glory to your Father who is in heaven" (Matthew 5:16). A Trailman begins to realize that the carefully crafted paths created by his parents, school, and home life will eventually end, and a new horizon will soon emerge. A Trailman who earns the Horizon Rank will have the amazing opportunity to "take the peak" of the entire Trail.

That peak is the **Freedom Award**.

The **Freedom Award** is the pinnacle award of Trail Life USA. A Trailman who earns this award experiences the wide-open range of his future. He is no longer called a "Trailman." He is now called a "Freedom Rangeman." He has the freedom to make his own decisions as a young adult experienced in accepting the consequences–good and bad–of his decisions. He has heard and learned about freedom found only in Christ. As a follower of Christ, he experiences freedom from the power of sin. "If the Son sets you free, you will be free indeed" (John 8:36).

Sword ●
Shield ●
Trail Life (TL) ●

● Trinity Peaks
● Stag
● Keys
● Cross
● Freedom

The symbols found in the Freedom Award image are powerful and have scriptural significance. The ●mighty stag is a rare creature that lives at the highest heights and exhibits strength and speed, beauty and grace. "He makes my feet like the feet of a deer: He causes me to stand on the heights" (2 Samuel 22:34 NIV). In C.S.Lewis' Narnia series, the white stag represents the Holy Spirit. In 1933, Lord Baden Powell, the founder of the global scouting movement, gave a farewell address centered around the stag as "the pure spirit of Scouting, springing forward and upward, ever leading you onward and upward to leap over difficulties."

The award also depicts ●two keys: one with a ●cross in the bitting cuts, and one with ●'TL' in the bitting cuts. These represent the work of the cross, as well as the influence of a Freedom Rangeman's

THE TRAIL LIFE STORY OF THE TRAIL 7

experience in Trail Life as essential in opening the doors a Trailman will encounter. "I will give you the keys of the Kingdom of Heaven" (Matthew 16:19).

The •Shield of Faith is drawn from Ephesians 6:16, "In all circumstances take up the shield of faith, with which you can extinguish all the flaming darts of the evil one;" reminding the Freedom Rangeman to continue to exercise his faith. It is red and covers a sea of blue, representing the blood of Jesus poured out for the "sea" of all of humanity. "We have fellowship with one another, and the blood of Jesus, His Son, purifies us" (I John 1:7 NIV).

The •Sword of the Spirit is a spiritual tool the Rangeman will use to guard his heart and defend his faith when under attack. "The sword of the spirit, which is the word of God" (Ephesians 6:17).

The •Trinity Peaks, present in all Adventurer ranks and the •Freedom Award, overarch and envelop them all, representing the omnipresent God the Trailmen and Rangemen serve, "May the grace of the Lord Jesus Christ, and the love of God, and the fellowship of the Holy Spirit be with you all" (2 Corinthians 13:14 NIV).

Special thanks to John Stemberger, Chairman of the TLUSA Board of Directors at its founding, for the first draft of this section.

what are the basics?

THE BASICS OF THE WOODLANDS TRAIL PROGRAM

The Woodlands Trail is the first part of an exciting journey for a boy in Trail Life USA.

It leads through the Woodlands with Steps, activities, and new skills that will prepare him for when he advances as a Navigator and, later on, an Adventurer. Eventually, the same trail he is on as a Woodlands Trail Trailman can take him to the peaks of a Freedom Rangeman—the highest achievement on the Trail Life trail.

It is helpful to understand where the Woodlands Trail program fits in the overall Trail Life USA program. The chart on the following page helps illustrate the structure and vision of the program.

WHAT ARE THE BASIC REQUIREMENTS FOR MEMBERSHIP IN TRAIL LIFE USA?

Membership in the program has both youth and adult elements. Youth membership in the program is open to all who meet the membership requirements, and is currently designed for biologically male children under the age of 18. The adult applicant must be at least 18 years of age and subscribe to and abide by the Trail Life USA Statements of Christian Faith and Values as well as the Oath and Motto of the program. While the program is undergirded by Biblical values and unapologetically reflects a Christian worldview, there is also a clearly defined inclusion policy for youth. Accordingly, all boys are welcome irrespective of religion, race, national origin or socio-economic status. HUMAN DIGNITY 3b Our goal is for parents and families of every faith to be able to place their boys in a youth program that endeavors to provide moral consistency and ethical

Trail Life
TROOP

Overseen by
TROOPMASTER

Woodlands Trail

5-10 YEARS
[Participation-based]

[Levels]
Fox
5-6 year-olds
↓
Hawk
7-8 year-olds
↓
Mountain Lion
9-10 year-olds
↓

Overseen by
RANGER

Program Philosophy
KNOWLEDGE

Available Awards
WORTHY LIFE AWARD (3)
TIMBERLINE AWARD

Navigators

11-13 YEARS
[Patrol Method]

[Core Skills Ranks]
Recruit Trailman
↓
Able Trailman
↓
Ready Trailman
↓

Overseen by
TRAILMASTER

Program Philosophy
UNDERSTANDING

Available Awards
WORTHY LIFE AWARD
RIDGELINE AWARD

Adventurers

14-17 YEARS
[Patrol Method]

[True Freedom Ranks]
Journey
↓
Ascent
↓
Horizon

Overseen by
ADVISOR

Program Philosophy
WISDOM

Available Awards
WORTHY LIFE AWARD
FREEDOM AWARD

Guidon

18-25 YEARS OLD
[Can be Co-Ed]

YOUNG ADULTS

Overseen by
COACH

Program Philosophy
LIFE

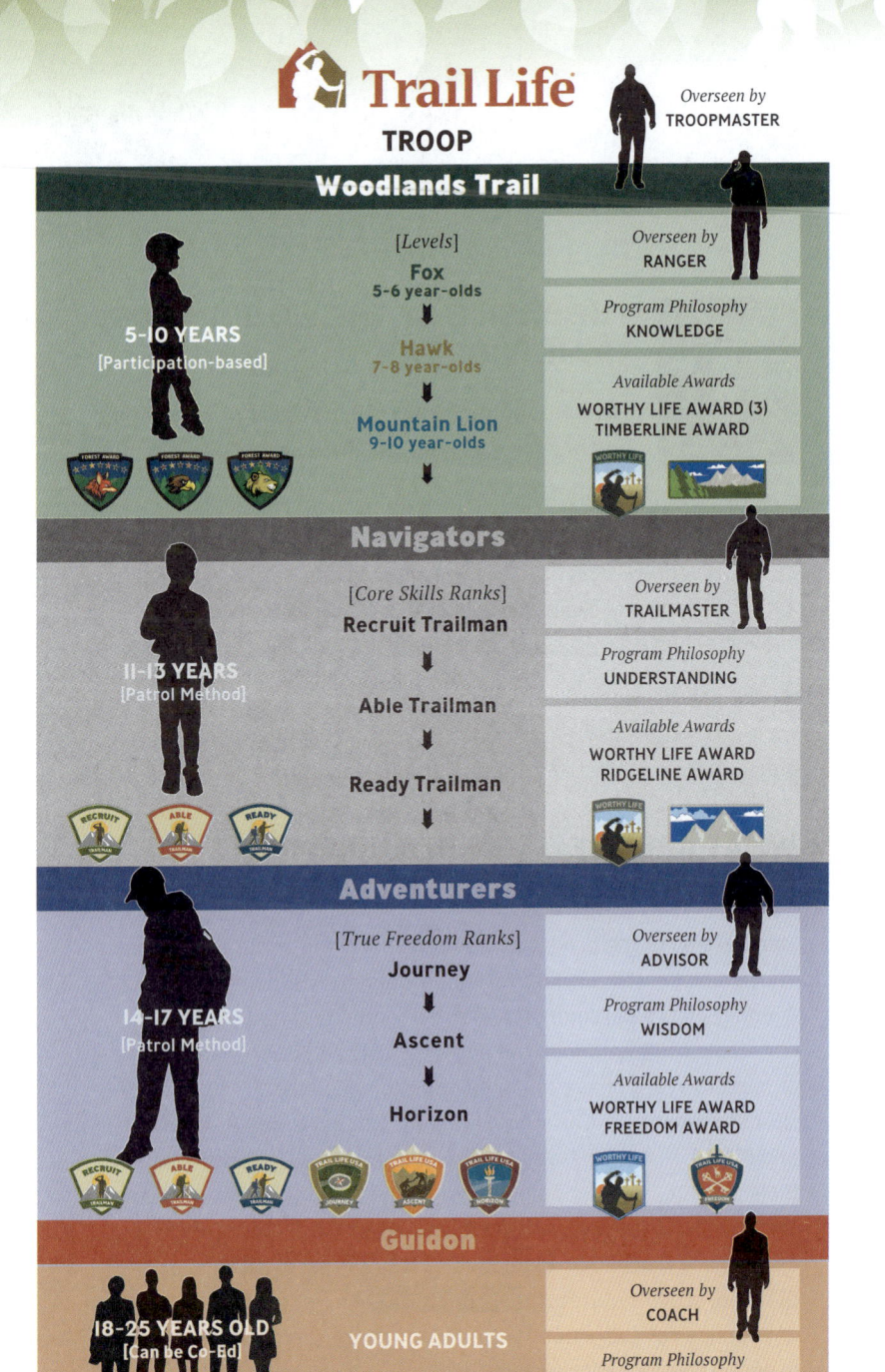

10 WOODLANDS TRAIL HANDBOOK

integrity in its adult leaders. Charter partners (usually churches) own and operate local Troops, selecting leaders and admitting members as they deem beneficial to their Troop and within the parameters of the organizational policy. The basis for the program's ethical and moral standards is found in the Bible.

Further information on Membership Standards can be found online.

membership

WHAT ARE THE SPECIFIC REQUIREMENTS FOR YOUTH MEMBERSHIP IN WOODLANDS TRAIL?

The program is designed that:

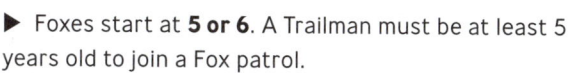

▶ Foxes start at **5 or 6**. A Trailman must be at least 5 years old to join a Fox patrol.

▶ Hawks start at **7 or 8**.

▶ Mountain Lions start at **9 or 10.**

Trailmen are expected to advance with other boys their age. Exceptions to the policy are allowed with a one-year variance, beginning with the Hawk patrol, in either direction (advancing or holding back) at the discretion of the Troop Committee. The Trail Life program is not based on academic benchmarks or maturity but on building relationships, spiritual growth, practical skill development, empathy and service, teamwork, and leadership. Boys develop in each of these areas at different rates. Some are natural leaders but need to develop teamwork. Some have mastered outdoor skills but need guidance on interpersonal skills. Regardless, advancing with boys their own age works best in Trail Life USA.

WHAT ARE THE BASICS? 11

WHAT ABOUT SAFETY?

Safety is everyone's business, from the most experienced Registered Adult leaders, parents, and guardians down to the newest youth member.

Any member adult encountered with the question, "Who is in charge of child safety and youth protection?" should confidently answer, **"I am!"** as we each have a role to play in protecting our boys.

All parents and adults are expected to be aware of the basic Youth Protection policies and orient their child as they see fit so everyone knows what is expected of Troop leadership and violations are addressed as needed.

Registered Adult leaders at all levels (including Registered Adults not assigned to specific roles) must undergo a criminal background check and complete the Child Safety Youth Protection Training (CSYPT) provided at registration prior to final approval of their membership.

CSYPT must be renewed every other year. This ensures all leaders remain current.

All Registered Adult leaders receive a Membership ID and lanyard which should be worn at ALL Troop meetings and events except when it may interfere with the safety of an activity. This ID reflects the volunteer's membership and

Adult lanyard

training expiration date. An adult leader may not participate in the program if their registration and training are not current.

12   WOODLANDS TRAIL HANDBOOK

1, 2, 3 YOUTH PROTECTION ESSENTIALS:

No One-on-one rule – A leader will never be alone with a youth Trailman unless they are a parent or legal guardian to that boy. This includes all supervision, communication, and transportation.

Two-deep Leadership – At least two Registered Adult leaders are required for supervision at every Trail Life function.

Buddy System of Three – Youth Trailmen should always remain with at least two other youth Trailmen for a total of three or more in a buddy group. A youth should never be alone at a Trail Life function nor can they be buddies with Trailmen from another program level (Navigators or Adventurers) unless they are siblings.

HERE'S A CONCISE EXPLANATION OF OUR TWO PRIMARY ACTIVITY POLICIES AND HOW THEY INTER-RELATE IN PRACTICE:

The No one-on-one rule is in place for youth protection so no boy is ever alone with an adult. This is for both the protection of the boy and the adult.

For gathering in individual rooms, single building locations at a larger facility, or vehicles transporting boys in the conduct of a Trail Life activity, there should never be an adult alone with a boy who is not his or her own son.

Generally speaking, **the Two-deep Leadership rule** is in place for *safety* so there is always a minimum of two Registered Adults in proximity to provide backup and oversight.

They should be within eyesight or earshot or both at all Trail Life gatherings and activities, with the recommendation being that, whenever possible, a minimum of 2 adults should be with every group of boys.

WHAT ARE THE BASICS?

Within the "No One-on-one" and "Two-deep Leadership" guidelines there is a targeted ratio of Registered Adult leaders to Woodlands Trail Trailmen at all age groups:

At least 2 Registered Adult leaders for up to 8 boys in the Fox patrol

At least 2 Registered Adult leaders for up to 16 boys in the Hawk patrol

At least 2 Registered Adult leaders for up to 20 boys in the Mountain Lion patrol and beyond

Leaders are trained to use the above policies, guidelines, and ratios to manage supervision during events and outings. Parents must defer to the leader's applications of these policies when accompanying their child unless clear violations of them are evident.

Detailed Child Safety Youth Protection Guidelines are available to all participants on Trail Life Connect.

WISDOM FOR USING TECHNOLOGY

If we were picking the most important inventions in the world, the internet would be a good choice. We use it to send messages, order Christmas gifts, do science projects, and even play games or watch movies. Although we are still discovering new ways to use digital technology for good, God-honoring purposes, the entrance of sin into the world has affected every part of creation. And not in a good way! This includes all forms of digital technology. Every day we discover new dangers, risks, and harmful effects that these kinds of technologies can bring.

Unfortunately, the online (or digital) world is also a place where ordinary people get attacked by thieves, predators, bullies, and criminal organizations. Many young people don't take that seriously until after they've been attacked themselves. This section is about helping you

to be safer in the way you use technology.

Be Careful.

Technology can make work easier, like a hammer or a motor does. But it can also be used against us without us knowing! So we need to be extra careful when we use it.

These Tools Have Risks.

If you misuse a hammer and hit a glass window, you can see ALL the damaging effects right away. The glass breaks. But if someone attacks you or steals from you on the internet, you might not know about it for years. And when you do find out, the damage may be deep and hard to fix.

Here are a few examples of how online technology can hurt you:

MEDICAL RISKS TO YOUR BODY

Sleep. Sun helps your body know when to feel awake or when to feel sleepy. The glowing screens of computers and cell phones act like sunlight. If you spend time looking at screens close to bedtime, that can keep you awake. And if it's a habit it can make you so tired your body can get sick.

Addiction. Just like with drugs, using digital technology releases a chemical in the brain that the brain wants more of. This can lead you to future addictive choices with even worse effects.

Tracker Mountain Lion

Passivity. Trailmen thrive on being physically active. Digital technology can keep us sitting around, playing games, or watching videos. Sitting around for a long time can change chemical levels in our bodies that make us not want to do anything. This can lead to us getting depressed and not being at our best in school, activities, or friendships.

RISKS TO YOUR SPIRIT

Tempting Pictures. The internet, movies, commercials, and apps are flooded with inappropriate pictures that can confuse the way we honor and respect other people, as well as cause addiction to seeing the pictures. This virtual world of pictures and things that aren't honoring to others or God can change our behavior and make it less likely that we will have healthy relationships with our friends and family.

Conscience. Looking at these images, or playing violent video games can change the way we feel about ourselves, too, as our conscience knows better and tells us that we did something wrong.

OTHER RISKS

Theft. Online identity theft is growing every day. Even a Trailman's friends could hack into each other's online accounts to steal identities and money. Many young people do not discover that they've been hacked until long after the theft.

Predators. Digital technology allows people you wouldn't let into your home to reach out to you. Many child abusers are hackers and know how and where you interact with technology.

TRAILMEN, LEARN TO PROTECT YOURSELF FROM THE RISKS.

OBEY. Follow your family's rules on when and how to use computers and phones.

USE DIGITAL SECURITY. For instance, use passwords that only you and your parents know. Don't share them with anyone else. Don't

make passwords too simple or they'll be easy to hack.

TALK TO YOUR PARENTS. Ask them about the dangers of digital technology. Ask them to help keep you safe and your identity secure.

FOLLOW THE TRAILMAN'S OATH

If a friend's parents are stricter than yours about technology, then obey the stricter rule when you're with that friend. The reverse is true, too. Don't ask your friend to watch the kind of movie that their parents don't allow or to view things or play games with your device that would cause them to disobey their parents.

FOLLOW YOUR TROOP RULES

Each Troop will make its own decisions as to what kinds of digital technology it allows as part of the Troop operations. Some Troops will forbid digital technology completely during Trail Life meetings and events. That may not be a bad idea!

To learn about what measures your Troop takes to protect Trailmen against the dangers posed by digital technology, ask your leaders. Additionally, to learn about specific technological risks and safety recommendations for particular activities, please find that particular activity in Trail Life's Activities Risk Reference Guide with the Health and Safety Guide on Trail Life Connect.

TALK WITH YOUR PARENTS ABOUT RESTRICTIONS

Your family may want to call a meeting to talk about this. Share this QR code with your parents if they want to find some more resources.

WHAT ARE THE BASICS? 17

TREAD LIGHTLY!®

Trail Life USA is a proud partner of *Tread Lightly!*® a non-profit organization founded by the National Forest Service. *Tread Lightly!*® promotes "responsible outdoor recreation through education."

IN THEIR WORDS...

Tread Lightly!® and its partners lead a national initiative to protect and enhance recreation access and opportunities by promoting outdoor ethics to heighten individuals' sense of good stewardship. *Tread Lightly!*®'s goal is to balance the needs of the people who enjoy outdoor recreation with our need to maintain healthy ecosystems and thriving populations of fish and wildlife. The scope of our work includes both land and water, and is representative of nearly every form of outdoor recreation including, but not limited to hunting, recreational shooting, fishing, and boating. We also have a niche in promoting safe and responsible use of motorized and mechanized vehicles in the outdoors.

TREAD PRINCIPLES

T **Travel Responsibly** on land by staying on designated roads, trails, and area. Go over, not around, obstacles to avoid widening the trails. Cross streams only at designated fords. when possible, avoid wet, muddy trails. On water, stay on designated waterways and launch your watercraft in designated areas.

R **Respect the Rights of Others** including private property owners, all recreational trail users, campers, and others so they can enjoy their recreational activities undisturbed. Leave gates as you found them. Yield right of way to those passing your or going uphill. On water, respect anglers, swimmers, skiers, boaters, divers, and those on or near shore.

E **Educate Yourself** prior to your trip by obtaining travel maps and regulations from public agencies. Plan for your trip, take recreation skills classes, and know how to operate your equipment safely.

A **Avoid Sensitive Areas** on land such as meadows, lakeshores, wetlands, and streams. Stay on designated routes. This protects wildlife habitats and sensitive soils from damage. Don't disturb historical, archeological, or paleontological sites. On water, avoid operating your watercraft in shallow waters or near shorelines at high speeds.

D **Do Your Part** by modeling appropriate behavior, leaving the area better than you found it, properly disposing of waste, minimizing the use of fire, avoiding the spread of invasive species, and repairing degraded areas.

TREAD LIGHTLY!® PLEDGE FOR KIDS

Travel only on trails

Respect animals, plants and people

Every time you go outdoors, think safety, bring a friend, and be prepared

Always leave the outdoors better than you found it

Discover how fun the outdoors can be when you tread lightly

You can find more educational materials for all ages and more about *Tread Lightly!*® on their website, www.treadlightly.org.

WHAT ARE THE BASICS? 19

TRAIL LIFE USA'S SIX ESSENTIAL CONCEPTS OF A CHRISTIAN WORLDVIEW

To assist Trailmen in thinking biblically about the lies of the world and the truths of God, Trail Life has developed Trail Life USA's Six Essential Concepts of a Christian Worldview that every Trailmen, both young and old, should learn. As you continue in Trail Life, you will notice that these concepts are integrated into every area of the Trail Life program. This intentionally serves to reinforce that God is part of everything we do.

1-TRUTH

1a There are absolute and unchanging truths about God and life.

1b Morality and moral law are absolute and unchanging because they proceed from and reflect God's unchanging nature and character.

1c A Trailman should show respect, understanding, and charity to others different from him, while maintaining firm Christian convictions.

2-CREATION

2a The eternal God created the universe for His purposes and according to His plan which is evident by the design, order and complexity found in all of creation.

2b All of God's creation is good. The entrance of sin into the world has affected every part of creation such that it is now fallen and imperfect.

2c Because man is sinful and imperfect, he is in need of salvation through Jesus Christ alone.

3-HUMAN DIGNITY

3a Out of all of God's creation, human beings are uniquely made in His image and likeness, and therefore all human life, from

20 WOODLANDS TRAIL HANDBOOK

conception through natural death has unquestionable value, worth, and dignity.

3b Because each human person is sacred and has intrinsic value, worth, and dignity, they should receive proper respect and protection regardless of age, disability, economic status, ethnicity, location, race, sex or sinful tendencies.

4-FAMILY

4a By His design, God created men and women different from each other and uniquely for His purposes.

4b God's design for marriage and family is that one man and one woman be united in marriage, and from that union, the blessing of new life comes forth.

4c Natural marriage which unites one man and one woman before God is an earthly reflection of God's Triune nature. Marriage also depicts the loving relationship between Christ and His church.

5-STEWARDSHIP

5a God has given all human beings dominion over His earth and commanded us touse its natural resources.

5b Therefore, each human being must be a good steward of the resources God provides and responsibly cultivate and conserve them for His glory.

6-PROVIDENCE

6a God is sovereign over all history.

6b God actively intervenes in peoples' lives for His purposes. He mysteriously uses all things, good and bad, for His glory.

6c God is good and can be trusted in all things.

You will notice in-line text *identifying Christian Worldview Essentials and subpoints referenced throught this handbook.*

WHAT ARE THE BASICS?

how does
the program work?

LEARNING IN THE WOODLANDS TRAIL PROGRAM

The Woodlands Trail curriculum is a 2-year course of study for Trailmen (boys) in each of the three age groups, called "patrols."

Foxes
(5-6 years old)

Hawks
(7-8 years old)

Mountain Lions
(9-10 years old)

Within the patrols, larger Troops may have several smaller patrols that are frequently named by the Trailmen.

Meeting plans revolve around a set curriculum to engage and teach program participants using six Program Emphases:

LEADERSHIP   FAITH

TEAMWORK   HERITAGE

CHARACTER   WISDOM

22 WOODLANDS TRAIL HANDBOOK

meetings

Meeting plans incorporate, directly or indirectly, the "Six F's":

FUN: This portion allows a time where Trailmen can burn off some energy. This is the time of the meeting for the Trailmen to play games or participate in a physical activity.

FOCUS: The Focus portion of the patrol meeting is to provide an academic or instructional element. This is the emphasis of the patrol time together to lay a foundation that the other F's will build upon.

FINGERS: This portion offers an opportunity for the Trailmen to experience a project with "hands-on" learning based on the Focus teaching segment. It is understood that boys learn to apply a lesson better when they can see and build or make something that would remind them of what is being taught.

FAITH: This portion of the meeting communicates pertinent biblical truths, values, and wisdom corresponding to the activity.

FAMILY: The Family portion of the meeting is simply the family emphasis for the principle taught. As the Trailmen learn throughout the years, it is the desire of Trail Life USA to inform and involve the family in the learning process as much as possible.

FOREST AWARD: Identifies the Branches taught and Steps focused on during a meeting for each age group.

'HIT THE TRAIL!' MEETING

While most of the meetings are indoors with a strongly-encouraged outdoors play option, Troops also conduct a monthly 'Hit the Trail!' meeting that includes an off-site activity, event, field trip, or community project.

HOW DOES THE PROGRAM WORK?   23

WOODLANDS TRAIL AWARDS OVERVIEW

Awards can be earned at all patrol levels along the Woodlands Trail. Award criteria are designed to be age-appropriate for the boy's cognitive and physical levels of development.

The primary areas of study in Woodlands Trail are the seven "Branches" (detailed on the following pages).

The Trail Guide presides over the patrol meeting and selects one Branch to work on at a time during the meetings. Each month, the learning portion of three weekly patrol meetings should center on the Branch Steps, with the fourth week being the 'Hit the Trail!' Activity.

THE AWARDS

When a boy joins any of the three Woodlands Trail program age patrols, he may earn the Fox, Hawk, or Mountain Lion "Branch Patch." This **joining patch** will be worn on the right pocket of the uniform and shows that the boy knows the basics of Trail Life USA, which include the oath, motto, salute, sign, and handshake. It is here he will attach Branch Pins as he progresses.

The Branch Pins correspond to the seven primary instructional areas of the Trail Life USA program for all ages. Branches in the Navigators and Adventurer programs are called "Frontiers."

Branch Pins are earned by completing Steps. **A Branch Pin will be given for each Branch completed the first program year.**

The color of the Branch Pin earned corresponds to the age group so that there is differentiation between Branches earned as a Fox (bronze), a Hawk (silver), and a Mountain Lion (gold).

Fox/bronze *Hawk/silver* *Mountain Lion/gold*

Fox Branch Patch with bronze pins  *Hawk Branch Patch with silver pins*  *Mountain Lion Branch Patch with gold pins*

the branches

Here is a helpful description of each Branch. The color indicates the color on the Branch Patch where a Trailman will attach his earned Branch Pin:

Heritage Branch (brown): An exploration of American Heritage, Christian Heritage, and a boy's own family heritage. Emphasis is placed on upholding the finest traditions of the heritage we obtain from our forefathers.

Life Skills Branch (burgundy): Teaching life lessons ranging from practical to higher-level interpersonal skill sets.

Science and Technology Branch (yellow): An exploration of physical and natural science concerning our created world.

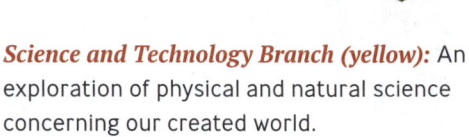

Hobbies Branch (black): An exploration of various indoor and outdoor hobbies that demand varying levels of knowledge, skill, or aptitude.

Values Branch (red): Instilling Bible-based values within the boys regarding any number of pertinent topics. The central focus of this Branch is teachings of the Christian faith.

Sports and Fitness Branch (green): Having fun in the outdoors with sports and other activities.

Outdoor Skills Branch (blue): Gaining basic understanding of woodcraft, hiking, exploration, and camping skills.

THE FOREST AWARD

The Forest Award is the target award for each Woodlands Trail patrol. It is earned upon completion of all 7 Branches, typically through the course of a program year. **This patch replaces the Branch Patch** on the right pocket of the Trailman's uniform. It is here he will attach his Sylvan Stars as he advances.

Fox Forest
Award

Hawk Forest
Award

Mountain Lion
Forest Award

The Forest Award, like the Branch patch, is set aside as a keepsake once the Woodlands Trail Trailman crosses over to the next level or the Navigators program.

WHAT IS A SYLVAN STAR?

A Trailman who receives his Forest Award is eligible to earn Sylvan Stars through continued participation in the program. One Sylvan Star is awarded for each Branch completed. The background embroidered Star colors on the Forest Award match the colors of the leaves on the Branch Patch.

The award representing each Sylvan Star earned changes with each age group so that there is differentiation between Stars earned as a Fox (bronze), a Hawk (silver), and a Mountain Lion (gold).

Fox/bronze

Hawk/silver

Mountain Lion/gold

SPECIAL AWARDS

Special awards are provided for completion of certain activities, projects, or accomplishments.

WORTHY LIFE AWARDS

The most important special award keeps the Trail Life USA program centered on faith. This is the Worthy Life Award. Requirements are different for the three different patrols.

On the Worthy Life Award, crosses can be earned at each program level, with the first cross presented along with the Award itself.

A Woodlands Trail Trailman can earn up to three crosses in his 6 program years. These crosses adorn the green ribbon. A fully-adorned Worthy Life Award will have 3 crosses on the green Woodlands Trail ribbon, one cross on the gray Navigators ribbon, and one cross on the blue Adventurers ribbon.

The Worthy Life Award is one of the awards that continues to be worn by the Trailman as long as he is a member of Trail Life USA.

The Worthy Life Award (pictured)
showing the maximum three crosses on the green Woodlands Trail
ribbon that can be awarded while in the Woodlands Trail program.

TIMBERLINE AWARD

The Timberline Award is the highest award a Trailman can achieve in the Woodlands Trail program and is available **only to Mountain Lion Trailmen.** It was developed to celebrate a boy's entrance into the new world of Trail Life USA's Navigators program.

Just as the tall timbers stop at the Timberline's edge, so must a Mountain Lion's time stop in the Woodlands Trail program. As the Trailman proceeds on his individual path, he leaves the Woodlands Trail and embarks on a new trail of exploration and experiences. The Trailman leaves with many good wishes and prayers that he will continue to Walk Worthy with the God Who created him, loves him, and guides him.

MANHOOD PRINCIPLES OF THE TIMBERLINE AWARD
(based on "Raising a Modern Day Knight" by Robert Lewis)

- **To live boldly and avoid being passive**

- **To live responsibly**

- **To lead courageously**

- **To live for the greater rewards of God**

TIMBERLINE REQUIREMENTS

To show that he is living boldly and is avoiding being passive he has:

1 Earned his Mountain Lion Forest Award

2 Earned all 7 Sylvan Stars (one from each branch) at the Mountain Lion level

3 Invited a friend that is a potential member to a Woodlands Trail meeting, outing, or activity.

4 Attended an overnight campout with the Troop during his Mountain Lion year(s).

To show that he is living responsibly he has:

Discussed, defined, and developed with his parents a plan to meet a measurable, quantifiable goal or fulfill an area of responsibility, and completed it for a minimum duration of 2 months. Requires prior approval of his Trail Guide. A goal might be improved physical fitness or improved academic success; an area of responsibility might be specific jobs or chores to do.

To show that he is leading courageously he has:

Helped plan and lead a service project in his community and enlisted help from his fellow Trailmen to complete it. His service project helped to make his community cleaner, better, safer, or fulfilled a need. Requires prior Trail Guide approval. Service exclusively to members of the Trailman's family are not eligible.

To show that he lives for the greater rewards of God he has:

Completed the Mountain Lion Worthy Life Award.

SUMMER MONTHS – "SUMMER ADVENTURE"

Summer meetings may consist of all ages, or a portion of the Troop as designated by the Troopmaster and Committee Chair.

If it is determined that Woodlands Trail will meet, Troops can plan an appropriate Summer Adventure for the Woodlands Trail Unit such as a day camp or overnight adventure. Wide latitude is given to the local adult volunteers for structure of these meetings and outings.

GUIDING TRAILMEN WITH SPECIAL NEEDS

God has specifically crafted every person with a unique personality, behaviors, and needs. Trail Life USA offers its boys and leaders structure and consistency, both of which are vital for boys with special needs. TRUTH 1c STEWARDSHIP 5a,b Please discuss any special needs with your Troop leadership, who can refer you to the volunteer committee that addresses advancement accommodations for special needs Trailmen.

where does
my son start?

THE WOODLANDS TRAIL BRANCH PATCH (JOINING AWARD)

A boy begins on the Trail by completing a set of **Joining Award requirements**. On completion, he earns the Branch Patch of his particular patrol (Fox, Hawk, or Mountain Lion), which must be earned before other awards are presented.

Families are encouraged to immediately assist their Trailman in achieving this award by focusing on the following requirements, then allowing the Trailman to demonstrate to the assigned Troop leader that he has mastered them. This is the beginning of a Trailman accepting and carrying out responsibility in Trail Life USA, a process that will be repeated over and over as he progresses, and the responsibilities increase in the challenge they provide.

Parents, as your Trailman completes his joining requirements, you can track his progress where indicated in this section; use the charts for his level in the Advancement Section beginning on 112—or for visual tracking at home, consider purchasing a Woodlands Trailmap for his level.

Fletcher Hawk

WOODLANDS TRAIL HANDBOOK

❙ **Memorize the Trailman Oath.**

The Trailman Oath is recited at the beginning of each meeting and at most gatherings. It is the shared commitment to traditional biblical values that binds all Trailmen.

> *On my honor, I will do my best*
> *To serve God and my country;*
> *To respect authority;*
> *To be a good steward of creation;*
> *And to treat others as I want to be treated.*

TRUTH Ic STEWARDSHIP 5a,b

Parents might want to review with their son the meaning behind the Trailman Oath. This will increase the impact of his commitment to live the Trail Life.

▶ *Oath* – An oath is a way of telling everyone how you want to live and what you are going to do.

▶ *"On my honor ..."* – On my honor means that you really mean what you are about to say and that you promise to do it.

▶ *"... I will do my best ..."* – When you do your best, it means that you will try as hard as you can until you can't try anymore.

▶ *"... to serve God ..."* – Serving God means that you obey what God tells you to do. The Bible is where we find what God wants us to do and not to do.

▶ *"... and (to serve) my country; ..."* – Serving your country means that you obey the laws (rules) like the speed limits and stop signs. It also means that you help others in your community.

▶ *"... to respect authority; ..."* – Respecting authority means that you listen, obey, and are kind to the people that are in charge, like parents, teachers, policemen, leaders, etc.

WHERE DOES MY SON START?

▶ ***"... to be a good steward of creation; ..."*** – Being a good steward of creation means that you will take care of the world that God made for you like it is a treasure. You do this by not littering, always trying to make things better, and using the things that God gives you wisely (not wasting anything).

▶ ***"... and to treat others as I want to be treated."*** – This means that you should think about how you want other people to talk to you and act towards you. Then you should talk to other people the same way and act the same way toward them.

REQUIREMENT 1 COMPLETED *(initial here):*

Boy _____ Parent/Guardian _____ Troop Leader _____

---

2 **Learn the Trailman Sign and when to use it.**

The Trailman sign is made with the right hand held open, palm forward, raising your right arm with your elbow at a right angle.

The sign is used during reciting of the Trailman Oath and is also used by Troop leaders as a signal to be silent.

If you see a Troop leader with his sign up standing quietly you should imitate him and see how fast the room goes silent!

REQUIREMENT 2 COMPLETED *(initial here):*

Boy _____ Parent/Guardian _____ Troop Leader _____

---

34 WOODLANDS TRAIL HANDBOOK

3 Learn the Trailman Salute and when to use it.

The Trailman Salute is made by raising your right hand. The tip of your fingers should almost touch your right temple or eyebrow. If you wear glasses, the tip of your fingers should almost touch the frames of your glasses. If you are wearing a Trail Life hat, the tip of your fingers should touch the brim.

A proper, crisp salute reflects well on your patrol and Troop. A sloppy salute does not properly honor the great traditions and hard work that went before. Practice bringing your hand up in one, smart motion and holding the salute until you are asked to drop it, then bring your hand directly down to its natural position at your side.

The Trailman Salute is used by Trailmen in uniform (defined by your Troop leaders) when:

- They recite the Pledge of Allegiance
- The flag passes in a parade or ceremony
- You are in a parade and pass the flag
- The flag is raised or lowered on a flagpole
- The national anthem is played or sung
- The flag is retired at flag retirement ceremonies

REQUIREMENT 3 COMPLETED *(initial here)*:

Boy _____ Parent/Guardian _____ Troop Leader _____

WHERE DOES MY SON START?

4 **Learn the Trailman Handshake.**

The Trailman Handshake is a forearm to forearm or wrist to wrist handshake.

This handshake was chosen because it is a strong way to assist another person in need.

REQUIREMENT **4** **COMPLETED** *(initial here):*

Boy _____ Parent/Guardian _____ Troop Leader _____

---

5 **Memorize the Pledge of Allegiance. (Fox can recite)**

I pledge allegiance to the flag
of the United States of America,
and to the republic for which it stands,
one nation under God, indivisible,
with liberty and justice for all.

REQUIREMENT **5** **COMPLETED** *(initial here):*

Boy _____ Parent/Guardian _____ Troop Leader _____

There is one more requirement if your son is joining as a Mountain Lion.

6 **Understand how to properly fold the American flag (Mountain Lions only).** *Your Troop leaders can assist in teaching this.*

REQUIREMENT **6** **COMPLETED** *(initial here)*:

Boy _____ Parent/Guardian _____ Troop Leader _____

Mom and Dad, you can begin tranferring these completed requirements to the charts in Chapter 6.

Bramble Fox

WHERE DOES MY SON ST

what do trailmen
wear?

THE TRAIL LIFE USA UNIFORM

A crisp unique uniform goes a long way in establishing a culture and creating identity within an organization. A Trailman is proud to display his uniform and achievements.

There are three distinct levels of uniforms within Trail Life USA. Participants in the Woodlands Trail should wear one of these three uniforms when participating in organized patrol or Troop events as directed by the Troop leadership.

All officially sanctioned uniforms are available at the online Trail Life USA store: *www.TrailLifeUSAstore.com*

- Questions regarding the proper display of uniforms should be resolved by the Trail Guide, Ranger, or Troopmaster.

- Trailmen should not wear torn or otherwise defaced or altered uniforms and should be neat in appearance.

- Closed-toed shoes are required.

The official **Trail Life USA Troop Uniform** is the preferred selection. It is the most formal uniform and is designed to display Troop and other identifying information as well as the awards of the Trailman. It consists of:

- Rip-stop fabric shirt
- Shoulder loops
- Troop number patch
- Rip-stop pants

- Web belt with embossed logo buckle
- There is no "official" uniform hat, but troops may require one.

38 WOODLANDS TRAIL HANDBOOK

The Troop Uniform is suitable for Troop meetings, field trips, award ceremonies, and fundraising.

The **Travel Uniform** is more formal than the Trail Uniform and is an option suitable for Troop or patrol travel, certain meetings, or events where the Formal Troop Uniform is not desired or would be impractical. It consists of the forest green Woodlands Trail collared shirt and Troop-approved pants. No awards are displayed on the Travel Uniform.

The **Trail Uniform** shirt is the least formal of the three uniform selections. It consists of the forest green Woodlands Trail T-shirt and Troop-approved pants. As its name implies, this informal uniform is suitable for hiking, camping, service project, or other outdoor event where comfort is key but Trailman identification is desired. No awards are displayed on the Trail Uniform.

Did you notice? Bramble, Fletch, and Tracker are wearing all three uniform types throughout this Handbook.

Troop Uniform

Travel Uniform

Trail Uniform

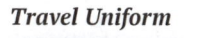

WHAT DO TRAILMEN WEAR? 39

UNIFORM AND INSIGNIA GUIDE

Trailmen wear their current level award (for Woodlands Trail, the Branch Patch or Forest Award) on their right pocket. They may wear a previously completed award patch on the left pocket, if they wish.

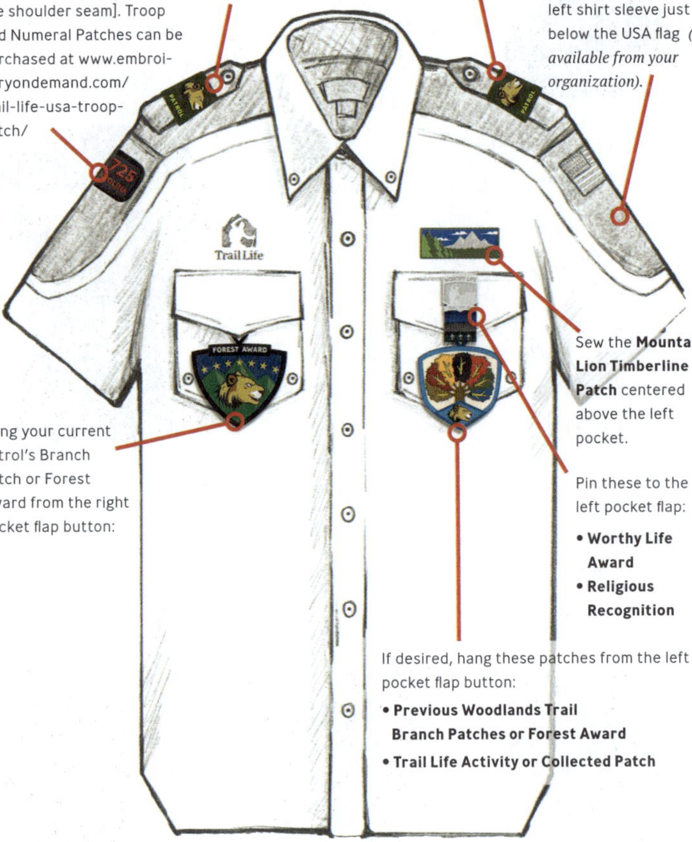

Sew the **Troop Numeral and State Patch** on the right shirt sleeve [l/4 in. below the shoulder seam]. Troop and Numeral Patches can be purchased at www.embroideryondemand.com/trail-life-usa-troop-patch/

Slide the appropriate **Shoulder Loops** for your patrol on to the shirt epaulette bars.

Sew an optional **Denomination/Faith Tradition Patch** on the left shirt sleeve just below the USA flag *(if available from your organization)*.

Sew the **Mountain Lion Timberline Patch** centered above the left pocket.

Hang your current patrol's Branch Patch or Forest Award from the right pocket flap button:

Pin these to the left pocket flap:
- **Worthy Life Award**
- **Religious Recognition**

If desired, hang these patches from the left pocket flap button:
- **Previous Woodlands Trail Branch Patches or Forest Award**
- **Trail Life Activity or Collected Patch**

40 WOODLANDS TRAIL HANDBOOK

how does a trailman
advance in his troop?

STEP SUMMARY

Branch Pins and Sylvan Stars (detailed in Section 3) are the primary advancement pieces that are awarded on the Woodlands Trail. They are affixed to Branch Patches or Forest Awards, depending on the Trailman's current advancement status within his patrol.

Branch Pins and Sylvan Stars are earned by completing a determined number of Core and Elective Steps in the seven color-coded Branches, as well as attending a 'Hit the Trail!' Activity or Troop outing for each Branch.

> In short, to earn a Branch Pin or Sylvan Star, a Trailman will complete the following in a particular Branch:
>
> 1. The required number of Core Steps, and
>
> 2. The required number of Elective Steps, and
>
> 3. One 'Hit the Trail!' Activity for that Branch.

Each program year and for each Branch, the Trail Guide chooses what to deliver from the Required Core and Elective Steps. For the Required Core Steps, keep in mind that any remaining Required Core Steps for that Branch would be delivered in the next year. Given the two years a Trailman remains in each level (Fox, Hawk, or Mountain Lion), he has the opportunity to complete all the Required Core Steps of every Branch in a two-year period before moving up to the next level. Steps can be completed at a meeting, campout, field trip, or other Troop or patrol gathering. Trailmen may receive only one

Branch Pin per Branch per level. Branch Pins are not transferable to the next level Branch Patch.

The Forest Award is earned by completing the 7 different Branches in a particular level. It must be earned before any Sylvan Stars may be awarded. Sylvan Stars are awarded in the same manner as Branch Pins. Trailman may receive only one Sylvan Star per Branch per level. Sylvan Stars are not transferable to the next level Forest Award.

'HIT THE TRAIL!' ACTIVITIES

'Hit the Trail!' Activities and outings are designed to broaden a Trailman's knowledge of his community and get him actively engaged in learning about service, outdoor activities, historic sites, exercise, community helpers, etc. It will prepare him for the increased involvement in his community as he pursues the Trail Life through Navigators and Adventurers in the future. Shared activities outside a meeting bond Trailmen together over time and shouldn't be neglected.

Your Trail Guide will consider local events like native American or other heritage festivals, sporting events, and art festivals in his annual program planning for 'Hit the Trail!' events. Perhaps you do something with your family that you can suggest. These activities are very much driven by the local Troop's community. And service can be incorporated into almost any Branch's activities, if desired. Patrols of different age groups (Fox, Hawk, or Mountain Lions) may plan these monthly outings together.

FAMILY HOME ACTIVITIES

Family Home Activities can be used to make up for missed patrol or Troop events. It is not the intent for the family to do all or even most of these activities (although families are welcome to do so, and we believe they will derive great benefit from the time spent together).

Family Home Activities explanation continues on page 44

REQUIREMENTS PER LEVEL

	Core Steps		Elective Steps		'Hit the Trail!' Activities
Heritage Branch					
Branch Pin	2	+	1	+	1
Sylvan Star	2	+	1	+	1
Hobbies Branch					
Branch Pin	1	+	2	+	1
Sylvan Star	1	+	2	+	1
Life Skills Branch					
Branch Pin	3	+	1	+	1
Sylvan Star	3	+	1	+	1
Outdoors Skills Branch					
Branch Pin	3	+	1	+	1
Sylvan Star	3	+	1	+	1
Science & Technology Branch					
Branch Pin	2	+	1	+	1
Sylvan Star	2	+	1	+	1
Sports & Fitness Branch					
Branch Pin	2	+	1	+	1
Sylvan Star	2	+	1	+	1
Values Branch					
Branch Pin	3	+	1	+	1
Sylvan Star	3	+	1	+	1

2 Family Home Activities = one Step or 'Hit the Trail!' per branch

7 Branch Pins Earned = Forest Award

HOW DOES A TRAILMAN ADVANCE IN HIS TROOP?

▶ **Two Family Home Activities** may be used to replace one missed Step or 'Hit the Trail!' Activity for each Branch Pin or Sylvan Star.

▶ **No more than one missed** Step or one 'Hit the Trail!' Activity per Branch or Sylvan Star may be replaced in this way.

▶ **All activities should be completed as a family** to the extent possible, but at minimum a parent or guardian and the Trailman should participate.

▶ **Trail Guides may suggest or allow other activities** not on the list for credit. They must be approved ahead of time.

▶ **The Trail Guide has the sole discretion for approving** participation in these activities for credit and may require discussion or documentation as he or she deems necessary.

▶ **Troops can provide a mentor** for boys who do not have the option of working through these with a family member or guardian. All Child Safety and Youth Protection Guidelines must be followed; see the Health and Safety Guide (online) for more information.

The following section describes the Core Steps and Electives organized by Branch.

Heritage Branch

[❷ Core Steps + ❶ Elective Step + ❶ 'Hit the Trail!' = **Branch Pin**]
[❷ Core Steps + ❶ Elective Step + ❶ 'Hit the Trail!' = **Sylvan Star**]

CORE STEPS *(2 required per year)*

1 Christian Heritage

Purpose: The 'Christian Heritage' Step provides a basic knowledge of the history of Christianity as documented in the Bible. Upon completion of this Step, Trailmen should be exposed to how some basic doctrines and traditions explained in the Bible apply to our Christian walk today.

During Troop meetings, Trail Guides will be working with the Trailmen to understand who Jesus is as well as other key biblical characters and stories such as the Christmas Story. Trailmen will also be learning about church heroes and martyrs that are not in the Bible, their stories, and their significance in the life of the church. TRUTH Ia Trail Guides will be instructing the Trailmen on prayer, namely how to pray and the importance of prayer.

Troops are free to shape these teachings with heritage facts from their own faith traditions.

2 Flag Etiquette and History

Purpose: The 'Flag Etiquette and History' Step provides a basic knowledge of the history and proper display of the United States flag. Upon completion of this Step, Trailmen should understand how to properly respect and display the flag.

During Troop meetings, Trail Guides will be teaching the Trailmen what the U.S. Flag currently looks like along with ways it has changed throughout the years. The Trailmen will also learn the meanings of the colors, stripes, and stars of the flag along with how to properly fold the flag. Trail Guides will also teach the Trailmen about the various parts and commands of a flag ceremony and the Pledge of Allegiance.

3 Founding Fathers

Purpose: The 'Founding Fathers' Step provides a basic knowledge of the men who helped draft the U.S. Constitution, Declaration of Independence, and lead the American Revolution. Upon completion of this Step, Trailmen should have heard about the motives, practices, and sacrifices of the founding fathers of our country.

During Troop meetings, Trail Guides will be helping the Trailmen study and learn at least three of the founding fathers, their education, and their sacrifices for America. The Trailmen will also learn how old these men were when they first made an impact on America and some of the ways that they impacted our country.

4 My Family

Purpose: The 'My Family' Step provides a basic knowledge of the variety of family size, structures, and relationships within the Trailman's own patrol. FAMILY 4a Upon completion of this Step, Trailmen should understand the importance of their own family and their important role as a member of their family.

During Troop meetings, Trail Guides will help the Trailmen learn what a family is and who the members of their own families are. Trail Guides will discuss with the Trailmen the importance of family traditions and some games and fun activities that the Trailmen have in their own families. The Trail Guides will also help the Trailmen understand the family roles and how they can sometimes change over time.

46 WOODLANDS TRAIL HANDBOOK

They will learn the importance of their own chores and how they help the family.

ELECTIVE STEPS *(1 required per year)*

5 My Community

Purpose: The 'My Community' Step provides a basic knowledge of the history and leadership of the Trailman's own local community. Upon completion of this Step, Trailmen should understand the importance of their community and its relationship with other surrounding communities.

During Troop meetings, Trail Guides will be working with the Trailmen to help them know the names of their local communities and how their community was named. Trail Guides will help them learn how to find their community and county on a state map as well as find local landmarks on a map, including: parks, the library, the fire station, their church, their house, the police station, and other local points of interest. The Trailmen will also learn who their local community leaders are and what they do along with recognizing an important historic event in their community.

6 Early America

Purpose: The 'Early America' Step provides a basic knowledge of the history of America prior to the formation of the United States. Upon completion of this Step, Trailmen should understand how life in early America was alike or different from life today as well as the motives, practices, and sacrifices of the European settlers.

During Troop meetings, Trail Guides will be working with the Trailmen to learn about the peoples that inhabited America before the arrival of European settlers and what life was like for them. Trail Guides will also teach who the pilgrims were and the importance of the

HOW DOES A TRAILMAN ADVANCE IN HIS TROOP? **47**

Mayflower. Trailmen will learn what the first Thanksgiving was like along with what the original 13 colonies were.

7 National Symbols

Purpose: The 'National Symbols' Step provides a basic knowledge of the various symbols and imagery associated with the United States. Upon completion of this Step, Trailmen should understand the importance, meaning, and history of these symbols and where they appear in our everyday lives.

During Troop meetings, Trail Guides will be working with the Trailmen to help them recognize some of our national symbols. Specifically they will understand what our national animal/bird symbolizes and be able to explain the different parts of the national seal. Besides the national symbols, Trailmen will learn about our national currency. They will learn the various symbols on our currency and the meaning and significance of "In God We Trust" on our currency. **PROVIDENCE 6c**

8 Armed Forces

Purpose: The 'Armed Forces' Step provides a basic knowledge of the five branches of the United States military. Upon completion of this Step, Trailmen should understand the differences, importance, and role of each branch.

During Troop meetings, Trailmen will learn about the five branches of the military and what they do. Trail Guides will also teach the Trailmen how to recognize the uniform for each branch and the differences and similarities between them all. They will examine the differences between their Trail Life USA uniforms and military uniforms. Trail Guides will instruct the Trailmen on some marching commands as well. The Trailmen will learn why it is important for soldiers to stay healthy and in shape. Trail Guides will help them to honor a veteran that they know personally.

48 WOODLANDS TRAIL HANDBOOK

9 American Culture

Purpose: The 'American Culture' Step provides a basic knowledge of the current culture and traditions of the United States. Upon completion of this Step, Trailmen should understand the variety of cultures and traditions that influence our lives, and the difference of American culture with the other cultures of the world. `TRUTH 1c` `HUMAN DIGNITY 3a,b`

During Troop meetings, Trail Guides will be working with the Trailmen to help them learn some things that are distinct to America. The Trailmen will also be able to distinguish between games that originated in America and games that originated in other countries. They will also discuss American and foreign foods. Trail Guides will also instruct the Trailmen on what it means to be a "melting pot" culture, and they will teach the Trailmen some common words that are taken from other languages.

10 My State

Purpose: The 'My State' Step provides a basic knowledge of the history and leadership of the Trailman's own state. Upon completion of this Step, Trailmen should understand the importance of their state, state symbols, and what sets it apart from other states.

During Troop meetings, Trail Guides will be working with the Trailmen to be able to recognize and know the distinctions of their own state flags. They will learn how to find their state on a U.S. map and recognize the states/countries/waters that border their state. The Trailmen will learn general information about their state such as their state symbols and items that are manufactured in their state. They will also learn who their current governor and state leaders are, as well as some famous people from their state and why they are famous.

HOW DOES A TRAILMAN ADVANCE IN HIS TROOP? 49

'HIT THE TRAIL!' ACTIVITIES *(1 required per year)*

Examples of activities your Trail Guide may schedule for the patrol for this Branch include visiting historic sites, monuments, buildings, and battlefields. Additionally, it may include local history fares, visiting with local government officials, visiting with veterans, or learning your community's history.

FAMILY HOME ACTIVITIES *(to replace missed Steps)*

For use if your Trailman should miss a meeting or 'Hit the Trail!' Activity. *(See details on pages 42 and 44.)*

Heritage Family Home Activities
for Fox Trailmen

Two may replace a missed Step or 'Hit the Trail!' Activity at the Trail Guide's discretion. See the complete guidelines at the beginning of this section.

☐ Visit a historical boat or tour the inside of a ship. Discuss the historical significance of that particular vessel or one like it.

☐ Pray daily for a week for the President of the United States and someone in the military.

☐ View the founding documents of the United States and explain something you liked about them.

☐ Discuss the voting process or look up your local and state elected officials.

☐ Learn about a family member who served in the military. If possible, look at pictures or memorabilia of their time in the service.

50 WOODLANDS TRAIL HANDBOOK

☐ Discuss those who have died for their faith. `PROVIDENCE 6a,b,c` This might include discussing martyrdom, sainthood, or missions, according to your beliefs and the level of depth you feel is appropriate. *Voice of the Martyrs* is a good resource if you need a starting point.

☐ Show examples of family trees, such as your own or of a Biblical character (Jesus). Create a simple family tree with at least three generations on it (child and siblings, parents, and grandparents). Bring the family tree to show your patrol at next meeting.

☐ Read a story about George Washington or another American patriot.

☐ Read and discuss a picture book about one of the Founding Fathers of our country. Make sure that you look at the pictures and discuss foods, homes, and other things that you see in them.

☐ Visit and explore a local, state, or national park.

☐ Attend an American holiday event such as a 4th of July celebration, Veteran's Day parade, historical reenactment, etc.

Heritage Family Home Activities
for Hawk Trailmen

Two may replace a missed Step or 'Hit the Trail!' Activity at the Trail Guide's discretion. See the complete guidelines at the beginning of this section.

☐ Take a driving tour of your community. Use a map to locate your church, school, park, library, fire station, and police station.

☐ Learn about a family member in the military. If possible, look at pictures or memorabilia of their time in the service.

☐ Participate in a food drive. Collect canned goods from home, friends, or neighbors to be donated to a local food bank/pantry or church food collection/distribution ministry. `HUMAN DIGNITY 3a,b`

HOW DOES A TRAILMAN ADVANCE IN HIS TROOP?   51

☐ Interview the oldest living family member you can contact, either in person or on the telephone. Some suggested questions: When and where were you born? What kinds of toys did you play with? What was school like? What was your favorite subject?

☐ Read and talk about the Navajo Code Talkers.

☐ Go and see, visit, or tour a historic boat or inside of a ship. Discuss the historic significance of the vessel.

☐ Visit and explore a local or national park. OR: Decide what you might do at a park, such as having a picnic or running races and do it in your backyard or living room. Report what was done with your Trail Guide.

☐ Attend an American holiday event such as a 4th of July celebration, Veteran's Day parade, historic reenactment, etc.

☐ Discuss men and women who have died for their faith. This might include discussing martyrdom, sainthood or missions, according to your beliefs and the level of depth you feel is appropriate for your child. PROVIDENCE 6a,b,c *Voice of the Martyrs* is a good resource if you need a starting point.

Heritage Family Home Activities
for Mountain Lion Trailmen

Two may replace a missed Step or 'Hit the Trail!' Activity at the Trail Guide's discretion. See the complete guidelines at the beginning of this section.

☐ Discuss how to care for our country's flag. Look up pictures of the evolution of the American flag.

☐ Decide on a service project your family can participate in together. HUMAN DIGNITY 3a,b Perhaps participate in a food drive. Collect canned goods from home, friends, or neighbors to be

52 WOODLANDS TRAIL HANDBOOK

donated to a local food bank/pantry or church food collection/ distribution ministry.

☐ As a family, do something for your neighbors: bake cookies as a gift, visit and ask about their favorite Christmas traditions and memories, sing Christmas carols, or help a neighbor with yard work.

☐ Learn about the election process. Visit a polling location or review a mail-in ballot/voter's guide.

☐ Visit a war memorial. Talk about what a memorial is and its importance. As a family, briefly pick up trash and clean around the memorial. Discover the history of the war commemorated by the memorial.

☐ Go and see or visit a boat or tour the inside of a ship and explore its history.

☐ Visit and explore a local or national park or decide what you might do at a park, such as having a picnic or running races, and do it in your backyard or living room.

☐ Attend an American holiday event such as a 4th of July celebration, Veteran's Day parade, historical reenactment, etc.

☐ Discuss men and women who have died for their faith. This might include discussing martyrdom, sainthood or missions, according to your beliefs and the level of depth you feel is appropriate for your child. *Voice of the Martyrs* is a good resource if you need a starting point.

family home activities

HOW DOES A TRAILMAN ADVANCE IN HIS TROOP?

Hobbies Branch

❶ Core Steps + ❷ Elective Step + ❶ 'Hit the Trail!' = **Branch Pin**
❶ Core Steps + ❷ Elective Step + ❶ 'Hit the Trail!' = **Sylvan Star**

CORE STEPS *(1 required per year)*

I General Hobbies

Purpose: The 'General Hobbies' Step provides a basic knowledge of the wide variety of hobbies and types of hobbies that exist. Upon completion of this Step, Trailmen should understand what a hobby is and become exposed to new hobby ideas they may find interesting. This Step serves to identify the remaining Steps for this Branch, allowing the Trailmen to choose based upon the collective interest of the patrol.

During Troop meetings, Trailmen will learn how to define a hobby and name several different types or categories of hobbies. The Trailmen will also be able to list examples of hobbies from the categories of Indoor, Outdoor, Collection, Competition, and Observation. The Trail Guides will also work with the Trailmen and their patrols to select two hobbies that their patrol will pursue at Troop meetings and one that their patrol will explore on a 'Hit the Trail!' gathering.

ELECTIVE STEPS *(2 required per year)*

HOBBY EXPERIENCE

Purpose: The intent of this Branch is to explore the activities and hobbies of interest to your Trailmen and to expose them to new

hobbies. The specific activity and questions to answer can vary greatly based on what is relevant to your Troop.

During Troop meetings, Trail Guides will work with the Trailmen to select an appropriate hobby. Here are general guidance questions that you may find helpful:

- What is the history/origin of the hobby?
- What special skills are needed for the hobby?
- What equipment is required for the hobby?
- What resources such as time, money, and materials are needed for the hobby?
- What separates professionals from amateurs in this hobby?
- What is the purpose of the hobby (entertainment, relaxation, competition, etc.)?

There are hundreds of hobbies. It would be a nearly impossible task to write Steps for each. Even if we tried, most assuredly, we would leave out many; and still others we could not do proper justice. These Steps should originate from the Trail Guides and local subject matter experts. There are several goals included in the Hobbies Branch:

▶ To expose boys to various hobbies that they would not normally have access to,

▶ To share their hobbies with fellow Trailmen and perhaps build deeper friendships due to shared interests,

▶ To strengthen interest in hobbies they already have, and

▶ To allow the Trail Guides, parents, or other experts to share interests with the boys.

CREATING HOBBIES BRANCH ELECTIVE STEPS

Trail Guides will use this as a guide to build their own Hobbies Branch Elective Steps for the patrol. To develop the activity plans they will follow the steps below. [C.L.E.A.R.] This process for developing an

HOW DOES A TRAILMAN ADVANCE IN HIS TROOP? 55

advancement of interest is an introduction to the format for opportunities the Trailmen will have to develop their own Trail Badges as Navigators and Adventurers.

C The patrol should **CHOOSE** a hobby that interests everyone in the patrol. *The patrol develops a list of options during Core Step 1. A list of example ideas is provided.*

L The step should include some opportunity to **LEARN** about the hobby. *This may cover aspects of the hobby such as equipment, rules, safety, history, etc.*

E The activity should **EXPLORE** some hands-on activities or skill building exercises related to the hobby. *These will obviously vary dependent on the hobby, but should be fun, engaging, and of a physical nature.*

A Each boy in the patrol should be given the opportunity to **APPLY** the skills developed and participate in the hobby using what he has learned. *These will obviously vary dependent on the hobby as it is the actual participation in the selected hobby.*

R The boys or patrol as a whole should **REPORT** or demonstrate what they have learned and/or experienced while participating in the hobby. *This should not be a term paper, or boring write up, nor just a simple discussion. This should be a fun, interactive opportunity for the boys to show off. Examples could be a hobbies fair, posters, video, picture collage, etc.*

'HIT THE TRAIL!' ACTIVITIES *(1 required per year)*

Some outings your Trail Guide might consider include active hobbies like sports, kite flying, hiking, or fishing. Other ideas include a patrol astronomy night, a museum visit, geocaching, bird watching, or possibly viewing private collections of art, cars, trains, fossils, etc. The possibilities are endless in hobbies!

SAMPLE HOBBIES LIST

Indoors/Casual	Outdoors	Collections	Competitions	Observations
3 D printing	Archery	Action figure	Airsoft	Aircraft spotting
Acting	Backpacking	Antiques	Animal fancy	Amateur astronomy
Amateur radio	Beekeeping	Antiquities	Archery	Amateur geology
Book restoration	Bird watching	Art	Billiards	Bird watching
Calligraphy	Camping	Book	Bowling	Bus spotting
Candle making	Cycling	Card	Boxing	Fish keeping
Computer programming	Fishing	Coin	Chess	Geocaching
Cooking	Flying disc	Comic book	Climbing	Herping
Cryptography	Fishing	Die-cast toy	Cycling	Hiking / back-packing
Digital arts	Gardening	Element	Dancing	Meteorology
Drama	Geocaching	Fossil hunting	Darts	Microscopy
Drawing	Handball	Insects	Debate	People watching
Electronics	Horseback riding	Metal detecting	Disc golf	Photography
Foreign language	Hunting	Mineral	Dog sport	Reading
Genealogy	Ice skating	Model Railroad	Equestrianism	Shortwave listening
Glassblowing	Inline skating	Movie and movie memorabilia	Exhibition drill	Train spotting
Juggling	Kayaking	Postcard	Fencing	Traveling
Leather crafting	KIte flying	Record	Field hockey	Whale watching
Lego® building	Metal detecting	Rock balancing	Fishing	
Origami	Orienteering	Sea glass	Gymnastics	
Painting	Paintball	Seashell	Laser tag	
Pottery	Photography	Stamp	Martial arts	
Sewing	Sand Art	Stone	Slot car racing	
Singing	Shooting	Video games	Swimming	
Soap making	Stone skipping	Vintage cars	Tennis	

HOW DOES A TRAILMAN ADVANCE IN HIS TROOP? 57

FAMILY HOME ACTIVITIES *(to replace missed Steps)*

For use if your Trailman should miss a meeting or 'HIt the Trail!' Activity. *(See details on pages 42 and 44.)*

Hobbies Family Home Activities
for Fox Trailmen

Two may replace a missed Step or 'Hit the Trail!' Activity at the Trail Guide's discretion. See the complete guidelines at the beginning of this section.

☐ Work together with your parent(s) to prepare, cook, and eat a special meal or dessert. Discuss with your parent(s) the things you enjoyed about this activity and why you enjoyed it.

☐ Spend time as a family engaged in an art project or watch a children's video about the life of an artist.

☐ Explore some careers in music.

☐ Explore a new hobby. Read a book on any new hobby that interests the whole family. At the next patrol meeting, explain what you found and what steps your family took to investigate this new hobby or start the new hobby.

☐ The Trailmen should ask their parents: Which service organizations you support, what those groups do, and why or how you chose to support them. TRUTH Ic HUMANDIGNITY 3a,b

☐ Discuss a service group or organization that focuses on one of your child's interests or hobbies.

☐ Make a list of historical places of significance in your town and make a plan with your parent(s) to visit at least one.

☐ Create a checklist of the 50 states and see if you can meet

58 WOODLANDS TRAIL HANDBOOK

someone from each state. Write their name and one interesting fact about them on your checklist.

☐ Discuss how to use a camera and take pictures together. Print some of the pictures and place in a photo album.

Hobbies Family Home Activities
for Hawk Trailmen

Two may replace a missed Step or 'Hit the Trail!' Activity at the Trail Guide's discretion. See the complete guidelines at the beginning of this section.

☐ Start a small collection or share information about the current collections of family members.

☐ Explore some careers in music.

☐ Have a "home" bird watch. Try to record up to 10 birds with simple observations. If time allows, research the type of bird on the Web. Always have a parent supervising when using the internet.

☐ Help your Trailman pack or make a list of his personal gear for a weekend camping trip (clothes, shoes, sleep gear, flashlight, first aid kit, mess kit, water bottle, etc.).

☐ Explore a new hobby together by researching it in books or online. Explain what you found to your patrol.

☐ Discuss how to use a camera and take pictures together. Print some of the pictures and place in a photo album.

HOW DOES A TRAILMAN ADVANCE IN HIS TROOP? 59

Hobbies Family Home Activities
for Mountain Lion Trailmen

Two may replace a missed Step or 'Hit the Trail!' Activity at the Trail Guide's discretion. See the complete guidelines at the beginning of this section.

☐ Work as a family to have a "home" bird watch. Try to record up to 10 birds with simple observations. If time allows, research the types of birds. Always have a parent supervising when using the internet.

☐ Talk about opportunities to spend time together in a positive and fun way. For example, have your family share hobbies or collections or, if a member of your family does not have a collection, you may start one! You may also spend time learning how to play checkers, chess, or another family game. This will give your family another positive way to spend free time.

☐ Discuss different hobbies that your family participates in. Is there a hobby you all share an interest in? Encourage each family member to have his or her own hobby to encourage individual identity and solitary time.

☐ Attend a performing arts event with your family or watch one on TV.

☐ As a family explore a new hobby. Research a new hobby that interests the whole family. At the next meeting, explain what you chose and what steps your family took to start the new hobby.

☐ Discuss how to use a camera and take pictures. Have your photos developed, or print them from your computer and place the pictures into a photo album or create a digital album.

60 WOODLANDS TRAIL HANDBOOK

Life Skills Branch

❸ Core Steps + ❶ Elective Step + ❶ 'Hit the Trail!' = **Branch Pin**
❸ Core Steps + ❶ Elective Step + ❶ 'Hit the Trail!' = **Sylvan Star**

CORE STEPS *(3 required per year)*

1 First Aid – Traumatic

Purpose: The 'First Aid - Traumatic' Step provides basic first aid knowledge for injuries that happen to a person. The Trailman should be able to detect injuries and be able to treat simple ones.

During Troop meetings, Trail Guides will teach the Trailmen about first aid and why it is considered "first." This training will include learning how to treat various injuries such as bleeding, fractures, sprains, bug bites or stings, and a foreign body. Most importantly, the Trailmen will learn when they need to call 9-1-1.

2 First Aid – Medical

Purpose: The 'First Aid - Medical' Step provides basic first aid knowledge for symptoms that happen within a body. The Trailman should gain a simple knowledge of the symptoms and how to treat them.

During Troop meetings, Trail Guides will teach the Trailmen about first aid and why it is considered "first." This training will include learning how to treat various medical conditions such as overheating, burns, hypothermia, and frostbite. The Trailmen will also learn how to recognize the symptoms of other major medical conditions such as heart attack, stroke, and shock. They will also learn how to respond and/or treat each major medical condition.

HOW DOES A TRAILMAN ADVANCE IN HIS TROOP?   61

3 Map Skills

Purpose: The 'Map Skills' Step provides a basic knowledge of what maps are and how they can be used. Basic features of maps will be understood. A Trailman should be able to find his general location on a map and how to get to another location.

During Troop meetings, the Trailmen will learn the differences between different types of maps and their specific uses. Based on ages, Trailmen will also learn the different features of a globe, world map, road map, USGS map, and hiking map. Trail Guides will also teach the Trailmen how an indoor floor plan is similar to a map.

4 Personal Safety

Purpose: The 'Personal Safety' Step should lead the Trailmen to be more aware of the world around them. It should teach them to see danger and to take appropriate action or avoidance.

During Troop meetings, Trail Guides will help the Trailmen learn how to be aware and secure in their surroundings. The Trailmen will learn how to recognize, avoid, and/or repair the dangers that are in or around their homes and meeting places. Trail Guides will instruct the Trailmen on what they should do if there is a fire in a building or if a person is on fire. The Trailmen will also be taught how medications and household cleaners should be safely stored. Most importantly, the Trailmen will learn how and when to call 9-1-1.

5 Stewardship

Purpose: The 'Stewardship' Step will teach the Trailman how to best use his time, money, and stuff. He will learn the value of work vs. time. He will learn that everything is really God's and he is a steward of what is God's. STEWARDSHIP 5a,b

During Troop meetings, Trail Guides will be instructing the Trailmen

on Stewardship. Trailmen will learn the definition of a steward as well as what it means to be a steward. Trail Guides will provide instruction on the best ways to steward one's time, money, and possessions.

6 Manners

Purpose: Manners play an important role in everyday life. They govern how to behave in public and private. They teach us to be considerate of others and how to act in various situations. The 'Manners' Step teaches how to consider others as we consider ourselves (Philippians 2:3).

During Troop meetings, Trail Guides will work with the Trailmen to learn what good manners are, their importance, and some important manners specific to Trailmen. `TRUTH Ic` `HUMAN DIGNITY 3b` The Trail Guides will also teach the Trailmen how to properly set a table and how to properly behave at a table. Trailmen will also learn general ways that they can help others as well as specific ways to show gratitude, such as when to write a thank you note.

ELECTIVE STEPS *(1 required per year)*

7 Water Safety

Purpose: The 'Water Safety' Step will teach the Trailman how to be safe in and around water.

During Troop meetings, Trailmen will learn the Trail Life USA safety guidelines for aquatics. They will learn the differences and meanings of the different swimming ability groups. Trail Guides will instruct the Trailmen on the four steps to rescue a drowning person. Most importantly, the Trailmen will learn how and when to call 9-1-1.

8 Home Maintenance

Purpose: The 'Home Maintenance' Step will teach Trailmen the importance of taking care of things. STEWARDSHIP 5a,b Preventative maintenance can help things last longer.

During Troop meetings, Trail Guides will instruct the Trailmen on the importance of home maintenance and the various people who can perform home maintenance tasks. Trailmen will know what home and car maintenance tasks are and which ones they can perform themselves. Most importantly, the Trailmen will learn how and when to call 9-I-I for a home maintenance emergency.

9 Animal Care

Purpose: The 'Animal Care' Step will teach the Trailmen about the responsibilities of owning pets and other animals.

During Troop meetings, Trailmen will learn about different types of pets and have an opportunity to share about their own or their friend's pets. The Trailmen will also learn about the types of food that pets eat, how to take care of them, and what to do with pets when they go out of town. Trail Guides will also teach the Trailmen about other animals that people own and how to care for those specific animals.

10 Gardening

Purpose: The 'Gardening' Step will teach the Trailmen how to prepare, plant, and grow a garden. The Trailmen should also understand that fruits and vegetables come from the ground, not just the store. STEWARDSHIP 5a,b

During Troop meetings, Trailmen will learn about the various types of gardens that people have and the reasons for planting those specific types. Trail Guides will also instruct the Trailmen on the steps and

64 WOODLANDS TRAIL HANDBOOK

importance of preparing a garden before planting. Trailmen will also learn how different types of plants should be planted and maintained.

11 Indoor Cooking

Purpose: The 'Indoor Cooking' Step will teach the Trailmen kitchen safety, the importance of menus, and how to follow a recipe.

During Troop meetings, Trail Guides will work with the Trailmen to understand ways to be safe in a kitchen. This includes learning about the different utensils and appliances and how they are used. Trailmen will learn helpful kitchen knowledge such as common cooking terms, how to measure different ingredients, what a menu and a recipe are, and the reasons to use menus and recipes. Trail Guides will also discuss the importance of using fresh foods.

12 Repairs

Purpose: The 'Repairs' Step will teach the Trailmen that repairing a broken object can save time and/or money over buying a new one. He should understand the satisfaction he will get from repairing something with his own hands. STEWARDSHIP 5b

During Troop meetings, Trail Guides will work with the Trailmen to understand the differences between repairs and maintenance. The Trail Guides will also discuss the advantages and disadvantages of repairing something and buying something new. The Trailmen will learn what things can be repaired and what items they can repair themselves.

'HIT THE TRAIL!' ACTIVITIES *(1 required per year)*

Suggested activities for your Trail Guide include delivering thank you cards to local community helpers at the police or fire station, hospital, or taking donations to an animal shelter. Service for others

HOW DOES A TRAILMAN ADVANCE IN HIS TROOP? 65

in the community such as at a nursing home, food pantry, or charity thrift store could be arranged—or even visiting the park or library to learn about everything you can do there. Woodworking, manners and etiquette, orienteering, or cooking classes all could be considered for 'Hit the Trail!' Activities.

FAMILY HOME ACTIVITIES *(to replace missed Steps)*

For use if your Trailman should miss a meeting or 'HIt the Trail!' Activity. *(See details on pages 42 and 44.)*

Life Skills Family Home Activities
for Fox Trailmen

Two may replace a missed Step or 'Hit the Trail!' Activity at the Trail Guide's discretion. See the complete guidelines at the beginning of this section.

☐ Discuss the value of sharing and pick a toy that the Trailman can give away.

☐ Have the Trailman interview his parents or guardians about friendship:
   a. How did you meet your childhood best friend?
   b. What do you like to do with your friends?
   c. What ideas do you have to help me make friends?

☐ Demonstrate how to buckle a seatbelt in the car. Try one of the following games or activities to pass the time in the car:
   a. The Alphabet Game
   b. Guess the Animal
   c. The License Plate Game
   d. Bingo
   e. I Spy

66 WOODLANDS TRAIL HANDBOOK

f. Coloring

g. Listen to music

h. Sing songs

i. Read a book

☐ Decide what budget you have to spend on food to donate to a local food pantry or other community organization. Go shopping for nonperishable items and deliver them to that organization. If your family's situation does not allow you to have funds to purchase extra items, ask your friends or neighbors if they will donate canned or boxed goods. Deliver the food to that organization.

☐ Review the Trail Life USA Child Safety Youth Protection Policy. Remind your son what to do in various situations. Let him know that he can always come to you with any concerns or issues that make him feel uncomfortable. Go online with your child to review other free material offered by NetSmartz, a site that focuses on youth protection.

family home activities

☐ Go on a hike at one of these locations:

a. State park

b. Wooded trail

c. Around your neighborhood

☐ Discuss Fire prevention and safety at home. Go to http://www. firesafekids.org/safety.html and learn about the three P's of fire safety.

☐ Cook a breakfast together using an easy recipe. Talk about different rules to follow when cooking in the kitchen. Discuss good hygiene practices and how to handle perishable foods.

HOW DOES A TRAILMAN ADVANCE IN HIS TROOP? **67**

☐ Take some time this week to review the rules your family has for walking in places you commonly visit. Consider some of these suggestions: do not run in a parking lot, walk in designated areas, stay at least three feet from parked cars, do not play in open parking spaces, always travel with a buddy or your parent, etc.

☐ Find an item in your home that you can reuse for another purpose. Work together to re-purpose that item.

☐ Discuss what kind of items you could pack in the car in case of emergencies. Create an emergency kit for your family car.

Life Skills Family Home Activities
for Hawk Trailmen

Two may replace a missed Step or 'Hit the Trail!' Activity at the Trail Guide's discretion. See the complete guidelines at the beginning of this section.

☐ Character is something that never changes, even when no one is looking. Take a few minutes tonight at bedtime to turn off the lights and let your imagination run wild with the shadows. Find fun, restful shapes out of the images you see and help your son develop his understanding that the character of an object does not change just because the lights have gone out.

☐ Each day for nine days choose a fruit of the Spirit (Galatians 5:22-23) and try to demonstrate that fruit during the day. **TRUTH Ib** At the end of the day, ask each family member how he or she exemplified that fruit of the day.

☐ Plan and help cook a meal as a family for two nights of the week. Sit at a table and have this meal together. Discuss healthy eating, the events of the day, or any other topic of interest. Have the Trailman set the table, remove the dirty items from the table, and clean the table.

☐ Spend time telling your family about some of your new friends. Make a poster that tells seven things about you to show the Trail Guide at the next meeting.

☐ Talk about ways to make new friends, ways to keep friends, and ways to stay safe when Mom & Dad are not with you.

☐ Try one of the following games or activities to pass the time in the car:
   a. The Alphabet Game
   b. Guess the Animal
   c. The License Plate Game
   d. Bingo
   e. I Spy
   f. Coloring
   g. Listen to music
   h. Sing songs
   i. Read a book

☐ Talk about Nutrition and Fitness and some goals for living a healthier lifestyle.

☐ Discuss the following:
   a. Importance of prayer
   b. Importance of teamwork
   c. Importance of planning
   d. Importance of doing your part to the best of your abilities

☐ Place five or six items in a bag that are significant to the Trailman. Examples include a small family photo, a favorite book, a souvenir from vacation, favorite pencil, favorite toy, etc. All items should be of the Trailman's choosing with parental approval. The boy should bring the bag and contents to show his patrol.

☐ Talk as a family about what it means to serve God and country and why we should have an Oath to do so.

HOW DOES A TRAILMAN ADVANCE IN HIS TROOP? 69

☐ Make a chart of emergency numbers. List parents' cell numbers as well as other emergency contact numbers to use if parents are not available. Make sure your Trailman knows your address and phone number. Play a memory game with him so that you are certain he knows them.

Life Skills Family Home Activities
for Mountain Lion Trailmen

Two may replace a missed Step or 'Hit the Trail!' Activity at the Trail Guide's discretion. See the complete guidelines at the beginning of this section.

☐ Evaluate and discuss your strengths and weaknesses as a listener. Set a goal to improve your listening skills.

☐ Discuss how to solve problems, especially when dealing with difficult people.

☐ Play a game with your family. Each family member writes down a personal strength or favorite activity on a slip of paper. Fold the papers and place them in a hat. Draw one at a time and try to guess which family member it is.

☐ Discuss the importance of goal setting with your family. Have your family share personal goals that they have made and achieved and maybe even some goals that they have not reached. Share the goal you created with your family and find a place to post your goal (like your refrigerator). Celebrate when you reach your goal.

family home activities

70 WOODLANDS TRAIL HANDBOOK

☐ With your family, discuss ways you can incorporate physical fitness into your family's routine. Implement this plan for 2 weeks.

☐ Raid your family's pantry! Discuss the food group each item belongs to and whether the item is a healthy food choice.

☐ Discuss the hazards of drug and alcohol abuse with your family.

☐ Learn how to use a compass. Use the compass to find landmarks or items to identify in your yard or house.

☐ Get a really good map of your neighborhood and practice your map-reading skills. Chart a planned route and determine the total distance. Travel your route (walk, drive, bike, etc.), and see how close your calculation was!

☐ Have a Family Meeting (dinner time is a good time) to discuss trust. How do we trust family members, and how do they trust us? Discuss why we trust parents to take care of children and how children earn parents' trust.

☐ Go over home safety. Go through the checklists and talk about keeping up with home safety and how the Mountain Lion can help do this. Discuss or determine the family escape plan in case of a fire or any emergency.

Outdoor Skills Branch

[❸ Core Steps + ❶ Elective Step + ❶ 'Hit the Trail!' = **Branch Pin**]
[❸ Core Steps + ❶ Elective Step + ❶ 'Hit the Trail!' = **Sylvan Star**]

CORE STEPS *(3 required per year)*

1 Ropes & Knots

Purpose: The 'Ropes & Knots' Step is to provide a basic knowledge and foundation of ropes and knots as tools. Upon completion of this Step, Trailmen should understand how to safely use ropes to perform basic functions.

During Troop meetings, Trailmen will receive introductory instruction on ropes and knots. This instruction will include learning about the various types of rope and their purposes. Trail Guides will also instruct the Trailmen on the different parts of the rope as well as how to properly care for a rope. Along with the rope instruction, Trailmen will learn some basic knots, their parts, and their usage. Trail Guides will also instruct the Trailmen on the best methods to "break" or untie each knot.

2 Orienteering

Purpose: The 'Orienteering' Step is to provide a basic working knowledge of land navigation in different environments. Upon completion of this Step, Trailmen should understand safe and reliable methods of land navigation.

During Troop meetings, Trail Guides will instruct the Trailmen on how to use a compass, how to use a map for orienteering, how to measure

72   WOODLANDS TRAIL HANDBOOK

distance while traveling, how to locate your position and direction on a map, and how to use directional techniques to guide you. Trailmen will also learn the different types and parts of compasses. Trail Guides will also explain the safety guidelines to follow while orienteering.

3 Outdoor Cooking

Purpose: The 'Outdoor Cooking' Step is to provide a basic knowledge of cooking and eating in an outdoor setting. Upon completion of this Step, Trailmen should understand how to properly prepare and cook meals under different circumstances.

During Troop meetings, Trail Guides will instruct the Trailmen on how to plan a menu for outdoor meals, properly prepare food in the outdoors, safely cook food outside, and properly dispose of food waste and trash in the outdoors. Trailmen will also learn what equipment is needed for outdoor cooking and how to best clean, sanitize, and store that equipment along with food in the outdoors. The Trailmen will also learn good hygiene practices for outdoors.

4 Camping & Hiking

Purpose: The 'Camping and Hiking' Step is to provide a basic knowledge of camping and hiking techniques. Upon completion of this Step, Trailmen should understand how to utilize commonly accepted camping techniques as well as understand basic hiking methods.

During Troop meetings, Trail Guides will work with the Trailmen on how to select a good campsite and properly lay out that campsite. Trailmen will also learn about the different methods of camping and the different types of tents. Trail Guides will instruct the Trailmen on how to properly take care of their tent. Trailmen will also learn and implement safety practices, good hygiene techniques, and common etiquette practices for outdoor activities.

5 Edge Tools / Woodsman Card for Mountain Lions

Purpose: The 'Edge Tools' Step is to provide a basic knowledge of edge tools. Upon completion of this Step, Trailmen should understand the dangers and the benefits of edge tools such as saws, axes, and knives. Mountain Lions will work toward earning their Woodsman card.

During Troop meetings, Trailmen will be exposed to various edge tools and the proper safety techniques when using them and being around them. Trail Guides will instruct the Trailmen on the uses for each particular type of edge tool, and Mountain Lions will experience using edge tools while pursuing their Woodsman Card. The Trail Guides will also cover the first aid techniques specific to cuts from edge tools.

6 Fire Safety / Fireguard Card for Mountain Lions

Purpose: The 'Fire Safety' Step is to provide a basic knowledge of fire. Upon completion of this Step, Trailmen should understand aspects such as fire safety, identification, and emergencies. Mountain Lions will work toward earning their Fireguard card.

During Troop meetings, Trailmen will learn the different types of fires and fire safety guidelines. They will also learn about various fire systems that are used along with fire drills and how to participate in them. Trail Guides will instruct the Trailmen on when and how to fight a simple fire and on first aid techniques involving burns. Mountain Lions will learn the Trail Life USA approved methods and rules for starting and maintaining a fire as part of pursuing their Fireguard Card.

ELECTIVE STEPS *(1 required per year)*

7 Fishing

Purpose: The purpose of 'Fishing' is to learn how fishing can provide food, entertainment, and relaxation.

During Troop meetings, Trailmen will learn the different areas, types, and methods of fishing as well as catch-and-release fishing. Trail Guides will help the Trailmen learn about fishing licenses. The Trailmen will learn whether or not they will need one and if an adult needs one. They will also learn about who oversees fishing activities. Trail Guides will teach the Trailmen about local fish, how to identify them, common fishing etiquette, and good safety practices for fishing.

`STEWARDSHIP 5a,b`

8 Tread Lightly!®

Purpose: The purpose of *Tread Lightly!*® is to learn that as stewards of this world, we are to take care of it and leave it no worse than how we found it.

During Troop meetings, Trail Guides will help the Trailmen understand what it means to *Tread Lightly!*® and why they should. The Trail Guides will instruct the Trailmen on the best practices of *Tread Lightly!*® Trailmen will learn what items can be left in the outdoors as well as what is to be done if something happens outdoors that cannot be undone. (*More about Tread Lightly!*® *on page 18*)

9 Tracking

Purpose: The purpose of 'Tracking' is to learn how small and unnoticed evidence can tell us so much about our surroundings.

HOW DOES A TRAILMAN ADVANCE IN HIS TROOP? 75

During Troop meetings, Trail Guides will teach the Trailmen about tracking, how it is used, and the benefits of tracking while camping/hiking. Trailmen will also learn about transference as well as how to identify certain animal prints.

10 Communications / Signaling

Purpose: The purpose of 'Communications/Signaling' is to learn that there are many ways that we can communicate with others and the world through simple technology around us.

During Troop meetings, Trail Guides will teach the Trailmen about communication devices that were used in the past and what they were used for. They will learn what type of messages each type of communication device sends and receives. Trailmen will also learn what communication devices can be used in the outdoors and what devices they can craft from nearby materials.

'HIT THE TRAIL!' ACTIVITIES *(1 required per year)*

Camping is the order of the day for this branch! It's the best way to get experience in all the outdoor skills. Additionally, Trail Guides may schedule day hikes, a day to visit a park or conservation facility, canoeing, or even a pioneering skill festival.

FAMILY HOME ACTIVITIES *(to replace missed Steps)*

For use if your Trailman should miss a meeting or 'HIt the Trail!' Activity. *(See details on pages 42 and 44.)*

76 WOODLANDS TRAIL HANDBOOK

Outdoor Skills Family Home Activities
for Fox Trailmen

Two may replace a missed Step or 'Hit the Trail!' Activity at the Trail Guide's discretion. See the complete guidelines at the beginning of this section.

☐ Practice the *Tread Lightly!*® policies at home. Do this by picking up after yourselves for one week. Take a walk around your yard and neighborhood to pick up trash you find. (*More about Tread Lightly!*® *on page 18.*)

☐ Make a 10 essentials pack for outdoor activities.

☐ Participate in a hike of at least ½ mile. Discuss how to be aware of your environment and what you enjoy about the outdoors.

☐ Go on an "I Spy" nature walk in your neighborhood. Sit outside for several minutes in silence. Write down what you see, hear, and smell.

☐ Set up a tent in your yard and make a list of the items you need to go on camping trip. Or go tent camping as a family.

family home activities

☐ Discuss good outdoor principles. Take a family hike and discuss and show how you can follow these principles correctly:

a. Travel on trails or other legal areas. Walk slowly on the trails. Respect the rights of others.

b. Respect animals, plants and people. Don't chase, scare, feed, or try to pet wildlife.

HOW DOES A TRAILMAN ADVANCE IN HIS TROOP? 77

c. Educate yourself – know before you go. Have a plan. Every time you go outdoors, think safety, bring a friend, and be prepared. Remember to pack the seven important items: water, food, first aid kit, raincoat or poncho, flashlight, sunscreen, and a whistle.

d. Always leave the outdoors better than you found it. Keep the outdoors clean! Don't litter or leave food behind. Pack it out and dispose of properly. STEWARDSHIP 5b

e. Discover how fun the outdoors can be when you *Tread Lightly!*®. Remember, the outdoors is home to many animals so treat it with care. Be careful with fire. (*More about Tread Lightly!*® *on page 18.*)

☐ Discuss Fire Safety in the outdoors.

a. We are good campers when we protect the homes of the animals around us by using fire safely.

b. Fox Trailmen should never start fires or play with lighters.

c. Keep area in fire circle (10' perimeter) clear of other items, and place tents a safe distance away from the fire.

d. We put fires out when not attended by an adult.

e. No horseplay in the fire circle.

f. Make sure to have water available in case the fire gets out of hand.

g. Do not put anything into the fire circle area without an adult's permission, including wood, marshmallows, and cooking sticks. (Some types of cones can pop and hot embers can fly out toward you.) Discuss the rule "What goes in the fire, stays in the fire."

☐ Do one of the following options:

a. Get out a real map and find your city or town. Find your street, your school, your church, your grocery store and other places you are familiar with on the map.

78 WOODLANDS TRAIL HANDBOOK

b. Get on the internet with your parent or guardian and look at your town as the satellite sees it from outer space. Can you see your house? What else can you identify?

☐ Take your Trailman to swimming lessons to strengthen his swimming ability.

☐ Build a canopy structure inside your home using tables, chairs, seat cushions, pillows, sheets, and blankets. Talk about how you were able to build the structure using everyday, ordinary objects. Allow your Fox Patrol member to sleep in the canopy structure. Take a picture of the structure to show your Trail Guide.

☐ Work with your parent(s) to cook one night's dinner outside and eat one dinner around a campfire. Work with your parent(s) to figure out how you are going to prepare the food, how you are going to cook the food, and how you are going to clean up the campfire area when finished..

Outdoor Skills Family Home Activities
for Hawk Trailmen

Two may replace a missed Step or 'Hit the Trail!' Activity at the Trail Guide's discretion. See the complete guidelines at the beginning of this section.

☐ Obtain a length of rope and instructions for two knots. Practice together and show your Trail Guide at next meeting.

☐ With assistance, the Trailman should fix something at home. This might be a piece of furniture, or a loose cabinet door, or to hang a picture on a wall.

☐ Prepare and eat fish for dinner one night. If possible, catch a fish or buy a whole fish to scale and fillet, or go to a market where you can watch the procedure.

HOW DOES A TRAILMAN ADVANCE IN HIS TROOP?   79

☐ With parent assistance, Trailmen should make a list of 8-10 items he needs to pack for a weekend camping trip. Obtain these items and organize in a bag or container.

family home activities

☐ Discuss the following with your Trailman:

a. **The buddy system:** This is a system of safety when out in the community, hiking, swimming or going anywhere. Teach your Trailman that his "buddy" can be a parent, sibling, friends at school, or a members of the Hawk patrol. Although it is important that we not teach children to be afraid of the world, they must be made aware that dangers exist and that it is important to always use the "buddy" system of three at Trail Life functions.

b. **Outdoor ethics:** When enjoying the outdoors, it is important to remember that the outdoors is the home of many creatures. It is up to all of us to preserve their world and keep it clean. We should never approach, feed, or try to pet animals in the wild. Lastly, we should remember to clean up any trash while enjoying the outdoors. STEWARDSHIP 5a,b Have the Trailmen present these guidelines to another family member.

☐ Participate in a hike of at least I mile. Discuss how to be aware of your environment and what you enjoy about the outdoors. While on a hike have the Trailman to use a compass to identify points of direction.

☐ Draw a treasure map of your yard or neighborhood or a park near your home. Make an "X" marks the spot on your map, and assist your Trailman in using the map to find the treasure.

80 WOODLANDS TRAIL HANDBOOK

☐ Develop a fire escape plan for your home and practice it, including removing screens, crawling through windows and down ladders from a second floor, and meeting at the designated location. Discuss escape plans from various locations in your home. Change smoke detector batteries, and listen to the sound that your smoke detector makes.

☐ Discuss and practice tornado, storm, hurricane, wildfire, and earthquake safety as appropriate to your location.

☐ Discuss what to do when lost in different situations:

- On a camping/hiking trip
- On a school field trip
- In the neighborhood
- At the park
- At the mall
- At a crowded event such as a fair, amusement park, community event

Outdoor Skills Family Home Activities
for Mountain Lion Trailmen

Two may replace a missed Step or 'Hit the Trail!' Activity at the Trail Guide's discretion. See the complete guidelines at the beginning of this section.

☐ Practice tying knots at home and teach someone different knots. Discuss the safety of not using knots to support your own weight or to climb into unsafe places, such as onto your roof.

☐ Discuss the importance of first aid in the home. Create or update a first aid kit for the house and place in a known, easily accessible location. If you already have a first aid kit at home, create one for the car or for camping.

☐ Visit the *Tread Lightly!*® website and discuss how you can incor-

porate the principles in your familiy activities. Find a spot to post your *Tread Lightly!*® pledge poster. (*More about Tread Lightly!*® *on page 18.*)

☐ Discuss the importance of taking care of the environment and being a good steward. Talk about ways you are good stewards and give examples. Discuss some areas in which you can improve. Make a goal and commit to changing your behavior. Post a reminder where you can see it each day. STEWARDSHIP 5a,b

☐ Look up how to make *pace counting beads* and make them. Learn how to pace count, and guide each other into finding your own pace numbers.

☐ Trailmen should pack their own gear for a weekend camping trip. Review what must and must not be included.

☐ Help your Trailmen look up how to use a compass. Practice by going outside and finding natural landmarks for them to identify. Get a really good map of your neighborhood and practice your map-reading skills. Chart a planned route and determine the total distance. Travel your route (walk, drive, bike, etc.), and see how close your calculation was!

☐ Participate in a 2-4 mile hike with your Trailman. Discuss how to be aware of your environment and what you enjoy about the outdoors. While on a hike, have the Trailman use a compass to identify points of direction.

☐ Plan and complete a scavenger hunt together. Discuss how team-work can help in accomplishing your goal.

Science and Technology Branch

> ❷ Core Steps + ❶ Elective Step + ❶ 'Hit the Trail!' = **Branch Pin**
> ❷ Core Steps + ❶ Elective Step + ❶ 'Hit the Trail!' = **Sylvan Star**

CORE STEPS *(2 required per year)*

1 Know Your Environment

Purpose: The 'Know Your Environment' Step provides a basic knowledge of outdoor elements that either benefit or hurt people through various types of contacts. Upon completion of this Step, Trailmen should understand that nature is not always safe and that learning identification and awareness is just the beginning of the journey.

During Troop meetings, Trailmen will learn about both beneficial and harmful plants that exist in their region of the country. They will also learn about both beneficial and harmful animals that live in their region. Trail Guides will teach the Trailmen how to recognize dangerous terrain and where it exists in their region.

2 Science in Weather

Purpose: The 'Science in Weather' Step provides a basic knowledge of meteorological conditions that affect our everyday lives. Upon completion of this Step, Trailmen should understand how weather affects us and ways in which you can use weather signs to help plan and prepare.

During Troop meetings, Trail Guides will instruct the Trailmen on the different types of clouds and precipitation. The Trailmen will learn what each type means and what specific things they need to know

about each one. The Trailmen will also learn about weather temperature and pressure, how they affect them and what they need to know regarding each.

3 Simple Tools and Machines

Purpose: The 'Simple Tools and Machines' Step provides a basic knowledge of what simple tools are and how they provide functionality in our everyday lives. Upon completion of this Step, Trailmen should understand the names and functions of the simple tools and have a few hands-on activities of each.

During Troop meetings, Trailmen will learn what each of the six simple tools are: Lever, Wheel, Pulley, Inclined Plane, Wedge, and Screw. The Trailmen will also learn how each tool is used and what it used for. The Trail Guides will provide hands-on activities where they can experience using and working with each item.

4 Astronomy

Purpose: The 'Astronomy' Step provides a basic knowledge of celestial objects and how they benefit us in various ways. Upon completion of this Step, Trailmen should understand many of the basic objects in the day and night sky and how to utilize these objects.

During Troop meetings, Trailmen will learn what each of the three major celestial bodies are: Sun, Moon, and Stars. The Trail Guides will provide instruction on how to recognize constellations and teach the Trailmen how constellations are used.

ELECTIVE STEPS *(1 required per year)*

5 Rocketry

Purpose: The purpose of 'Rocketry' is to learn how this science has propelled our advancement in technology. Also, to understand that this is one of many areas where math can be fun.

During Troop meetings, Trailmen will learn the different parts of a rocket and the different types of fuel that a rocket uses. Trail Guides will work with the Trailmen to make sure that they understand the safety procedures that are used in rocketry and also help them in making a simple, safe rocket. Trailmen will also learn how rocketry has benefited mankind.

6 Ancient Weapons

Purpose: The purpose of 'Ancient Weapons' is to learn about how older weapons furthered mankind's understanding and knowledge through survival and adversity.

During Troop meetings, Trail Guides will teach the Trailmen about various ancient weapons that have advanced technology. Trailmen will explore some of the uses of these technologies and learn when they were first used. Trail Guides will instruct on how to be safe around these technologies and work with the Trailmen to build a simple and safe ancient weapon.

7 Improvised Tools

Purpose: The purpose of 'Improvised Tools' is to learn that tools are everywhere, and crafting simple tools can be useful when camping or hiking.

During Troop meetings, Trailmen will learn about what types of tools have been crafted throughout history as well as what tools can be

crafted from outdoor materials. Trail Guides help the Trailmen learn how to find good basic materials for crafting, how to be safe using crafted tools, and how to make a simple crafted tool.

8 Botany

Purpose: The purpose of 'Botany' is to learn and understand more about trees and plants. Identification can be a great asset while camping or hiking.

During Troop meetings, Trail Guides will help the Trailmen to understand botany and its related areas of study. Trailmen will also learn about plants that are local to their area and how to identify them. The Trail Guides will also help the Trailmen know which of their local plants are dangerous, beneficial, or neither.

'HIT THE TRAIL!' ACTIVITIES *(1 required per year)*

Trail Guides will have numerous options for planning opportunities for Trailmen to observe and interact with Science and Technology in the community. Science museums, planetariums and observatories, nature trails, local wildlife centers, science fairs, robotics competitions, and radio or television station tours are all examples of what is possible for the Science and Technology 'Hit the Trail!' Activities.

FAMILY HOME ACTIVITIES *(to replace missed Steps)*

For use if your Trailman should miss a meeting or 'HIt the Trail!' Activity. *(See details on pages 42 and 44.)*

86   WOODLANDS TRAIL HANDBOOK

Science and Technology Family Home Activities
for Fox Trailmen

Two may replace a missed Step or 'Hit the Trail!' Activity at the Trail Guide's discretion. See the complete guidelines at the beginning of this section.

☐ Look up the weather forecast. Answer some of the following questions:

   a. What is the weather supposed to be like tomorrow?
   b. What is it like for the next week?
   c. Is any rain or snow forecasted?
   d. Is it going to be cloudy or clear?
   e. Is it going to be hot, cold, or comfortable?

☐ Discuss the potentially dangerous weather condition(s) in your community. Make a plan for safety precautions and procedures with these conditions.

☐ Review and discuss with your family the Wisdom for Using Technology section of this Handbook *(see page 14)*. Discuss your family's technology policies.

☐ Have each family member present choose one plant that he or she would like to have in your yard or home and requirements for it to thrive. Purchase at least one of the choices and plant or place appropriately.

☐ Choose new fruits and vegetables to try. Help prepare them for a meal.

☐ Do one of the following options:

   a. Draw a picture of your pet or a pet you would like. What color is its fur? What color are its eyes? Does it have long fur or short? Is its tail long or short?

HOW DOES A TRAILMAN ADVANCE IN HIS TROOP? **87**

b. Ask your parent or guardian if he or she had a pet as a child. Ask your parent or guardian to tell you some stories about the pet.

c. Feed your pet for a week.

d. Watch a movie about an animal.

family home activities

☐ Smell the different aromas of herbs and spices in your kitchen. Create a blind-folded smell and/or taste test for family or friends with different common spices/scents (vanilla, garlic, cinnamon, etc.).

☐ Look up three stars/constellations visible in your night sky and find them on a night walk.

☐ Read Genesis 1 and 2; discuss the biblical account of creation.
CREATION 2a

Science and Technology Family Home Activities
for Hawk Trailmen

Two may replace a missed Step or 'Hit the Trail!' Activity at the Trail Guide's discretion. See the complete guidelines at the beginning of this section.

☐ Find a video online of a plane breaking the sound barrier and discuss what happens when a plane breaks the sound barrier.

☐ Place a seed cup in a well-lit window and watch it daily for two weeks. Water the plant as needed. Discuss the growth and development of the seed. Or plant or maintain a family garden.

☐ Look up the insects in the Bible, and draw a line from the insect to the listed scripture.

SCRIPTURE	INSECT
Matthew 6:19-20	Ant
Deuteronomy 7:20	Bee
Proverbs 6:6	Caterpillar
Exodus 16:19-20	Fly
Exodus 8:21	Gnat
Judges 14:8	Hornet
Psalms 78:46	Locust
Deuteronomy 28:38	Moth
Matthew 23:24	Worm

☐ Spend some time in your yard. Look for the parts of an ecosystem in your yard (soil, water, plants/trees, decomposers, animals).

☐ Look up three stars/constellations you can see from your location. Take a night walk and find them.

☐ Take a hike and allow the Trailman to use the compass to identify points of direction.

☐ Read Genesis 1 and 2; discuss the biblical account of creation.
CREATION 2a

☐ Find and view a video clip of "Punkin Chunkin'" from the Science Channel and talk about the different kinds of catapults.

☐ Discuss the three types of rocks, their characteristics, and what is the most commonly found in your area.

☐ Talk about the animals that you would see in your neighborhood or at the homes of friends and family. If your family has a pet, have your Trailman to be responsible for feeding, watering, and caring for your pet for a week.

☐ Track and chart the weather for at least five days including:

- **Temperature** (Was it warmer, cooler, or the same as yesterday?)

- **Wind** (Was it calm or windy? What was the direction of the wind?)

- **Precipitation** (Was it rainy or dry?)

- **Clouds** (What type of clouds do we see?)

☐ Discuss the potentially dangerous weather condition(s) in your community. Make a plan for safety precautions and procedures with these conditions.

Science and Technology Family Home Activities
for Mountain Lion Trailmen

Two may replace a missed Step or 'Hit the Trail!' Activity at the Trail Guide's discretion. See the complete guidelines at the beginning of this section.

☐ Find a video online of a plane breaking the sound barrier and explain what happens when a plane breaks the sound barrier.

☐ Discuss other science topics in creation with your family. Talk about how God reveals Himself to us.

☐ Discuss astronomy and astronomy careers.

☐ Observe the weather for one week by recording basic elements such as the predicted temperature, the actual temperature,

sunrise, sunset, precipitation, etc. Watch the weather on TV, or look at the chart in your newspaper.

- [ ] Look up instructions and make your own crystals or rock candy.

- [ ] Discuss the importance of keeping trash off the ground to prevent animals and insects from getting in. Do a quick clean up around your yard or inside your house. Be sure to look for anything that may attract bugs (food wrappers, spills that need to be wiped up, etc.).

- [ ] Discuss biodegradation of items and the seriousness of problems caused by non-biodegradable waste.

- [ ] Discuss pulleys, and try to find them in use around your house (for example, on the front of your car's engine).

- [ ] Discuss levers and inclined planes. Try to find them in use.

- [ ] Discuss construction of structures with your family. Visit different locations of interest from a safe distance to see construction in action.

- [ ] Discuss the potentially dangerous weather condition(s) in your community. Make a plan for safety precautions and procedures with these conditions.

family home activities

Sports and Fitness Branch

[**2** Core Steps + **1** Elective Step + **1** 'Hit the Trail!' = **Branch Pin**
2 Core Steps + **1** Elective Step + **1** 'Hit the Trail!' = **Sylvan Star**]

CORE STEPS *(2 required per year)*

1 Nutrition & Fitness

Purpose: The 'Nutrition & Fitness' Step covers the general physical well-being for the Trailman. He will learn the difference between healthy and unhealthy foods, some of the physical issues with eating poorly, and exercises to keep fit.

During Troop meetings, Trailmen will learn how to define nutrition, and they will learn its importance. Trail Guides will explain which foods provide good nutrition and which foods provide poor nutrition. Trailmen will also learn what illnesses are associated with poor nutrition. Trail Guides explain the different types of fitness and explain why they are important. Trailmen will learn and practice various ways to stretch their muscles and joints as well as different exercises that will make them healthier, stronger, and/or faster. Trail Guides will work the Trailmen to set fitness improvement goals.

2 Learn about Sports

Purpose: The 'Learn about Sports' Step teaches the Trailman about the wide variety of sports and how to train for them. He will also learn how to be a good sport.

During Troop meetings, Trailmen will discover the vast number of sports that exist and discuss several. They will learn the differences

92 WOODLANDS TRAIL HANDBOOK

between team sports and individual sports. Trail Guides will teach the Trailmen how to train for various sports and explain the importance of practice and training. Trailmen will also learn about and practice being a good sportsman.

CREATING SPORTS AND FITNESS BRANCH ELECTIVE STEPS

The Elective Steps should be created by the Trail Guide. There are a wide range of sports to select from and even many fitness events to participate in. Trail Guides will use the **C.L.E.A.R.** Method to develop these Elective Steps. This process for developing an advancement of interest is an introduction to the format for opportunities the Trailmen will have to develop their own Trail Badges as Navigators and Adventurers.

C The patrol should **CHOOSE** a sport or fitness activity to teach.

L The step should include some opportunity to **LEARN** about the sport. *This may cover rules, strategy, history, etc.*

E The activity should **EXPLORE** some hands-on activities or skill building exercises related to the sport. *These will obviously vary depending upon the sport, but should be fun, engaging, and be of a physical nature.*

A Each boy in the patrol should be given the opportunity to **APPLY** the skills developed and participate in the sport using what he has learned.

R The boys or patrol as a whole should **REPORT** or demonstrate what they have learned and/or experienced while participating in the hobby. *This should not be a term paper, or boring write up, nor just a simple discussion. This should be a fun, interactive opportunity for the boys to show off.*

SAMPLE SPORTS ELECTIVE STEPS *(1 required per year)*

3 Uncommon Sports

Purpose: The 'Uncommon Sports' Step will expand the knowledge base of sports to the Trailman. He will learn about sports from across the globe and perhaps enjoy playing one.

During Troop meetings, Trail Guides will discuss with the Trailmen some uncommon/unusual and old fashioned games and sports. Trailmen will learn how they are played and why people enjoy playing them. Trailmen will also have the opportunity to experience playing one or more of these uncommon sports.

4 Soccer *(sample team sport)*

Purpose: The 'Soccer' Step will teach the Trailman the rules, strategy, and skills of this sport.

During Troop meetings, Trailmen will learn the rules and purpose of this sport. Trail Guides will teach the Trailmen about the different positions and what exercises one needs to do to get better at this sport. Trailmen will also learn the benefits of this sport.

5 Bowling *(sample individual sport)*

Purpose: The 'Bowling' Step will teach Trailman basic rules and skills of this sport.

During Troop meetings, Trailmen will learn the rules and purpose of this sport. Trail Guides will teach the proper scoring method(s) for this sport and some of the different skills and exercises needed to perform well and the benefits of this sport.

6 **Swimming** *(sample sport)*

Purpose: The 'Swimming' Step will teach Trailman a basic understanding on safety and skills needed for this sport.

Trail Guides will discuss with the Trailmen the difference between competitive swimming and swimming as a skill. They will discuss different strokes used for different reasons and the etiquette and rules of swimming in pools and other water sources. Safety around the water is the key lesson with Swimming.

'HIT THE TRAIL!' ACTIVITIES *(1 required per year)*

Baseball games in the summer or hockey games in the winter, watching or playing sports or other fitness activities are easy to come by everywhere. Fun runs, swimming holes, sledding, bike rodeos, or hiking are all great ways for the patrol to have fun together at the Sports and Fitness 'Hit the Trail!' event.

FAMILY HOME ACTIVITIES *(to replace missed Steps)*

For use if your Trailman should miss a meeting or 'HIt the Trail!' Activity. *(See details on pages 42 and 44.)*

Sports and Fitness Family Home Activities
for Fox Trailmen

Two may replace a missed Step or 'Hit the Trail!' Activity at the Trail Guide's discretion. See the complete guidelines at the beginning of this section.

☐ Ask family members if they participated in sports or fitness activities. Listen to the stories and ask two questions at the end of the story. Some suggestions are:

   a. What was their most difficult experience playing a sport?

   b. What did they learn by playing?

   c. What was their best memory?

☐ Take a hike around your house. See how many things you can find that are related to sports and fitness. Examples include: pictures, magazines, books, sports equipment, awards, outdoor goals, trampoline, etc. Discuss the benefit of physical activity in your daily life.

☐ Complete a bike safety check on all bikes before going on a bike ride of at least 30 minutes. Example: check for reflectors, brake function, correct tire pressure, helmet fit, etc.

☐ Do one of the following options as a family:

   a. Go outside and play in a water hose or sprinkler.

   b. Play a board game.

   c. Make up a game and teach it to a sibling, parent or guardian, or grandparent.

☐ Talk about what it means to be a good sport when winning and losing. Play a game where everyone demonstrates good sportsmanship. TRUTH 1c HUMAN DIGNITY 3b

96 WOODLANDS TRAIL HANDBOOK

☐ Go on a hike of at least 30 minutes.

☐ Participate in a formal race event (i.e. swimming, running, biking or obstacle course).

☐ Look up good meals or foods to eat before sports activities. Eat one before doing a family fitness activity.

Sports and Fitness Family Home Activities
for Hawk Trailmen

Two may replace a missed Step or 'Hit the Trail!' Activity at the Trail Guide's discretion. See the complete guidelines at the beginning of this section.

☐ Discuss with family members if they participated in sports when they were young. Listen to stories about their experience and ask two questions at the end of the story. Some suggestions are:

   a. What was their most difficult experience playing a sport?

   b. What did they learn by playing?

   c. What was their best memory?

☐ Discuss the benefit of physical activity in your daily life. Make an exercise plan for a week and follow it.

☐ Complete a bike safety check on your family's bikes. Take a bike ride of at least 30 minutes. Example: check for reflectors, brake function, adjust tire air pressure, etc.

☐ Do one of the following options:

   • Play in a water hose or sprinkler.

   • Play Frisbee or another active outdoor activity.

   • Talk about what it means to be a good sport when winning and losing. Act out some examples of good and bad sportsmanship.

HOW DOES A TRAILMAN ADVANCE IN HIS TROOP?   97

☐ Go on a hike at one of these locations:

    a. State park

    b. Wooded trail

    c. Around your neighborhood

☐ Participate in a formal race event (i.e. swimming, running, biking or obstacle course).

☐ Look up pre-participation meals or sports nutrition on the internet and write down a good meal or foods to eat before sports activities. Eat one before a family fitness activity.

Sports and Fitness Family Home Activities
for Mountain Lion Trailmen

Two may replace a missed Step or 'Hit the Trail!' Activity at the Trail Guide's discretion. See the complete guidelines at the beginning of this section.

☐ Learn a new sport or participate in a fitness activity regularly together.

☐ Review the *Tread Lightly!*® pledge with your family on a hike or walk. (*More about Tread Lightly!® on page 18.*)

Travel only on trails

Respect animals, plants and people

Every time you go outdoors, think safety, bring a friend and be prepared

Always leave the outdoors better than you found it

Discover how fun the outdoors can be when you tread lightly

☐ Review and discuss boating safety with your family.

98 WOODLANDS TRAIL HANDBOOK

☐ Participate in a sports activity with your family.

☐ Discuss at least four character traits you think a great sportsman should have.

☐ Talk about what it means to be a good sport when winning and losing. Practice being a good sport when you are playing sports or other games. TRUTH 1c HUMAN DIGNITY 3b

☐ Go on a hike of at least a mile and a half.

☐ Participate in a formal race event (i.e. swimming, running, biking or obstacle course).

☐ Look up pre-participation meals or sports nutrition and write down a good meal or foods to eat before sports activities. Eat one before a family fitness activity.

☐ Play outside for at least 30 minutes three times in a week.

☐ Review and discuss bicycle safety. Have the Trailmen review with their parents what they learned and check their own equipment including helmets and proper clothing to be worn while biking. Go on a bike ride of at least 30 minutes.

family home activities

☐ Talk about safe swimming and what should be done as a family to keep everyone safe. Go over the **13 Points of Safe Swimming** from The American Red Cross (below) before you head out to the pool or beach:

- Swim in designated areas supervised by lifeguards.

- Always swim with a buddy; do not allow anyone to swim alone.

HOW DOES A TRAILMAN ADVANCE IN HIS TROOP? 99

- Never leave a young child unattended near water and do not trust a child's life to another child; teach children to always ask permission to go near water.

- Have young children or inexperienced swimmers wear U.S. Coast Guard-approved life jackets around water, but do not rely on life jackets alone.

- Maintain constant supervision.

- Make sure everyone in your family learns to swim well.

- If you have a pool, secure it with appropriate barriers. Many children who drown in home pools were out of sight for less than five minutes and in the care of one or both parents at the time.

- Avoid distractions when supervising children around water.

- If a child is missing, check the water first. Seconds count in preventing death or disability.

- Have appropriate equipment, such as reaching or throwing equipment, a cell phone, life jackets, and a first aid kit.

- Know how and when to call 9-1-1 or the local emergency number. (**If you are swimming at a lake, be sure to look this up before traveling, and know the name of the lake area (ie. East Bay, Cove 3, etc.) so that rescue teams can find you.)

- Protect your skin. Limit the amount of direct sunlight you receive between 10:00 a.m. and 4:00 p.m. and wear sunscreen with a protection factor of at least 15.

- Drink plenty of water regularly, even if you're not thirsty. Avoid drinks with alcohol or caffeine in them.

© *Copyright The American National Red Cross. All rights reserved.*

Values Branch

[**3** Core Steps + **1** Elective Step + **1** 'Hit the Trail!' = **Branch Pin**]
[**3** Core Steps + **1** Elective Step + **1** 'Hit the Trail!' = **Sylvan Star**]

CORE STEPS *(3 required per year)*

1 Godly Values

Purpose: The 'Godly Values' Step provides a basic knowledge of what Values are and the benefit of having and living by values based on godly principles. TRUTH Ia,b,c Upon completion of this Step, Trailmen should understand where our values come from and why they are important.

During Troop meetings, Trailmen will learn how to define what a value is and name some values. Trail Guides will help the Trailmen understand how values affect our lives and some of the places that we get our values from. They will learn the importance and benefits of having godly values in their lives.

2 Our Faith

Purpose: The 'Our Faith' Step provides a basic knowledge and understanding of what faith is and its practical application. Upon completion of this Step, Trailmen should understand how we can utilize our faith to serve and help others around us as well as the biblical foundation of lasting faith and the importance of placing one's faith in God who is trustworthy. PROVIDENCE 6a,b,c

During Troop meetings, Trail Guides will help the Trailmen understand what faith is and why it is of the utmost importance that we

HOW DOES A TRAILMAN ADVANCE IN HIS TROOP?

place our faith/trust in Jesus. Trailmen will learn how our faith is affected by our values. Trail Guides will lead discussions with the Trailmen on examples from the Bible where a value is specifically defined.

3 Godly Citizenship

Purpose: The 'Godly Citizenship' Step provides a basic introduction to the concept of a Christian worldview and how the Trailman can influence their world in a positive godly direction. Upon completion of this Step a Trailman should understand how his actions influence his community and his witness. TRUTH Ic

During Troop meetings, Trailmen will learn what it means to be a godly citizen and how to interact with the world with a Christian worldview and what that means. Trailmen will learn what the actions of a godly citizen are like and how they can be involved in our government, school, and community as part of being a godly citizen.

4 Service

Purpose: The 'Service' Step provides a basic knowledge of what service is and its benefits to the giver and receiver. Upon completion of this Step, Trailmen should understand the importance of service to God and others.

During Troop meetings, Trail Guides will teach the Trailmen how service is defined and why it is good to perform service. Trailmen will learn who they can serve, and they will discuss examples of what is considered community service for Trail Life USA. Trail Guides will help the Trailmen learn that service not only benefits others but themselves as well. Trailmen will learn what it means to serve God as stated in the Trailman Oath. Trail Guides will lead discussions about examples from the life of Jesus that demonstrate and encourage us to be servants.

102 WOODLANDS TRAIL HANDBOOK

5   Teamwork

Purpose: The 'Teamwork' Step provides a basic knowledge of the principles and value of working as a team. Upon completion of this Step, Trailmen should understand, through experience, the challenges and benefits of team activities and the importance of cooperation.

During Troop meetings, Trail Guides will help the Trailmen define teamwork and understand why it is important. The Trailmen will learn various activities that depend on teamwork such as sports, school, jobs, etc. The Trail Guides will also teach the importance of cooperation when it comes to completing a task or goal and teach how to recognize things that can interfere with both cooperation and teamwork.

6   Truthfulness/Integrity

Purpose: The 'Truthfulness/Integrity' Step introduces the Trailman to the concept of always being trustworthy in what you say and do. Upon completion of this Step, Trailmen should understand the importance and practical application of this character trait. `TRUTH Ib,c`

During Troop meetings, Trail Guides will help the Trailmen define truthfulness and integrity and understand why it is important in their lives. Trail Guides will lead discussions with the Trailmen about times in their lives when their truthfulness or integrity was tested. Trailmen will also learn what can be done to regain trust once it has been lost. Trail Guides will also lead discussions about how the Trailman's friends can influence his truthfulness and integrity in both positive and negative ways.

ELECTIVE STEPS *(1 required per year)*

7   Courage

Purpose: The 'Courage' Step introduces the Trailman to the concept

of action despite one's fears. Upon completion of this Step, Trailmen should understand the importance and practical application of this character trait.

During Troop meetings, Trail Guides will help the Trailmen define courage and understand why it is important. Trailmen will learn examples of courage found in the Bible and throughout history. Trail Guides will lead discussions with the Trailmen about ways that they have shown courage in their own lives and how showing courage helps those around them.

8 Obedience

Purpose: The 'Obedience' Step introduces the Trailman to the concept of learning to follow. Upon completion of this Step, Trailmen should understand the importance and practical application of this character trait.

During Troop meetings, Trail Guides will help the Trailmen define obedience, learning to follow, and understand why it is important. The Trailmen will learn how obedience helps them become a better leader, honors God, and shows respect for authority. Trail Guides will also work with the Trailmen to help them recognize areas in their own lives where they need to improve their obedience.

9 Righteousness

Purpose: The 'Righteousness' Step introduces the Trailman to the concept of Biblical right living despite one's situation or surroundings. Upon completion of this Step, Trailmen should understand the importance and practical application of this character trait.

During Troop meetings, Trail Guides will help the Trailmen define righteousness and understand why it is important. Trail Guides will help the Trailmen know what the right way to live and act is in various circumstances. The Trail Guides will also explain how the

Bible provides a consistent standard for living despite one's situation or surroundings. The Trailmen will learn how certain activities such as prayer, Christian fellowship, Bible study, etc. can help them build an understanding of Biblical right living. The Trailmen will also learn practical ways that they can encourage others to be and live righteously. Most importantly, the Trail Guides will help the Trailmen to understand how the sacrifice of Jesus Christ makes us righteous in the eyes of a Holy God. **TRUTH 1a,b** **CREATION 2b,c**

10 Wisdom

Purpose: The 'Wisdom' Step introduces the Trailman to the concept of knowing what to do and how to use one's knowledge. Upon completion of this Step, Trailmen should understand the importance and practical application of this character trait.

During Troop meetings, Trail Guides will help the Trailmen define wisdom as knowing what to do and how to use one's knowledge and understand why it is important, especially as leaders. Trail Guides will help the Trailmen know some different places to gain wisdom, namely the Bible, experiences, studies, and trustworthy guidance among others. The Trailmen will learn how to recognize examples of wise and unwise decisions. The Trail Guides will lead discussions about historical leaders and followers that showed wisdom such as Solomon, Daniel, George Washington, etc.

11 Dedication

Purpose: The 'Dedication' Step introduces the Trailman to the concept of being committed to something and not quitting. Upon completion of this Step, Trailmen should understand the importance and practical application of this character trait.

During Troop meetings, Trail Guides will help the Trailmen define dedication and understand why it is important to persevere through hardship. The Trailmen will learn the ways that our dedication to God

is shown and grows when we are persecuted for our faith. The Trail Guides will help the Trailmen to recognize areas in their own lives where their dedication can improve. The Trail Guides will also lead discussions about historical figures and groups that showed great dedication such as Helen Keller, Christian martyrs or missionaries, and the Navy Seals. PROVIDENCE 6a,b,c

12 Repentance

Purpose: The 'Repentance' Step introduces the Trailman to the concept of being sorry and changing one's actions and attitude. Upon completion of this Step, Trailmen should understand the importance and practical application of this character trait.

During Troop meetings, Trail Guides will help the Trailmen define repentance and understand why it is important. CREATION 2b,c The Trail Guides will lead discussions with the Trailmen about times in the Trailman's lives when he realized that he was going the wrong way or doing the wrong thing, stopped, and turned around. The Trailmen will learn what it takes to repent, according to their faith tradition. The Trail Guides will also lead discussions about historical figures that have shown repentance such as Saul of Tarsus (Apostle Paul).

13 Respect Life

Purpose: The 'Respect Life' Step introduces the Trailman to the idea that God created him in His own image for a purpose and he is fearfully and wonderfully made. CREATION 2a HUMAN DIGNITY 3a,b Upon completion of this Step, Trailmen should understand the importance and practical application of this truth.

During Troop meetings, Trail Guides will lead discussion and activity related to how God lovingly and carefully molded the Trailman in His own image and knew all about him in his mother's tummy. Trailmen will learn that image is more than skin deep, can be distorted by sin, and how Jesus perfectly lived and reflected the ideal image of God.

Trail Guides will help the Trailmen identify the ways God uniquely made each of them for His purposes. PROVIDENCE 6a,c

'HIT THE TRAIL!' ACTIVITIES *(1 required per year)*

Whether visiting a nursing home to sing Christmas carols or cleaning the church for Easter, service and giving back to others is often the focus of the Values 'Hit the Trail!' event. Additionally, See You at the Pole, National Day of Prayer, vacation bible school, Christian speakers, or other church events may be considered for Values 'Hit the Trail!' Activities for the patrol.

FAMILY HOME ACTIVITIES *(to replace missed Steps)*

For use if your Trailman should miss a meeting or 'HIt the Trail!' Activity. *(See details on pages 42 and 44.)*

Values Family Home Activities
for Fox Trailmen

Two may replace a missed Step or 'Hit the Trail!' Activity at the Trail Guide's discretion. See the complete guidelines at the beginning of this section.

☐ Do something nice for a neighbor: bake cookies as a gift, visit neighbor, sing Christmas Carols, or help a neighbor with yard work, for example.

☐ Darken the room and light one candle. Note how one little light brightens the entire room. Discuss how a person's integrity ("doing what is right and saying what is true") is like a light to family members and friends.

HOW DOES A TRAILMAN ADVANCE IN HIS TROOP? 107

☐ Talk with your family about respecting others and understanding differences and individuality. **HUMAN DIGNITY 3a,b** Discuss how we can show our "inward" character traits of respect and responsibility. For several days, choose a household chore (picking up your laundry, helping with the dishes) that you can do to show responsibility.

☐ Do a family service project. Talk to your Trail Guide for ideas of projects appropriate for Fox Trailmen.

☐ Spend some time looking at photos that include family members and friends of all generations. Talk about these individuals and share your stories of them with your children. Thank God together in prayer for the family that he has given you.

☐ Make homemade Christmas cards or gifts to give to each other for Christmas. Spend time on Christmas Eve or Christmas Day giving these gifts to one another and giving thanks for one another.

family home activities

Values Family Home Activities
for Hawk Trailmen

Two may replace a missed Step or 'Hit the Trail!' Activity at the Trail Guide's discretion. See the complete guidelines at the beginning of this section.

☐ Talk to your parents about what it means to honor them. Show them that you love them by doing a chore without being asked.

☐ Plan and help cook a meal with your family. Sit at a table and have this meal together. Discuss healthy eating, the events

of the day, or any other topic of interest.

- [ ] Think about some practical ways you can serve your family this week. Help your mom with housework, do a task for your dad that you notice he's been too busy or too tired to do, or arrange to spend time with a grandparent for the afternoon.

- [ ] Food Drive—Help those in need! **HUMAN DIGNITY 3a,b** Participate in a food collection effort. Collect canned goods from home, friends, or neighbors. You can use allowance to purchase canned food items. Ask friends and neighbors to donate non-perishable food items, personal toiletry items, or baby food items.

- [ ] During a family meal this week, have each family member tell why they are thankful for each of the other family members.

- [ ] As a family, do something for a neighbor: bake cookies as a gift, visit the neighbor, sing Christmas carols, or help a neighbor with yard work.

- [ ] Call a grandparent or another beloved adult and talk about ways you can show honor to the adults in your life. Practice holding the door open for the ladies and girls in your family.

- [ ] Watch a movie together about Joshua and the Battle of Jericho or another biblical leader.

- [ ] Have a family discussion about values. What values do parents believe are most important? What values do the Trailman believe are most important? **TRUTH 1a,b** Discuss ways these values can be demonstrated in your daily lives.

- [ ] Ask your parents to help you find the North Star at night. Tell them the story of how a star guided the wise men to baby Jesus. Discuss how Jesus can guide us through life.

HOW DOES A TRAILMAN ADVANCE IN HIS TROOP?   109

Values Family Home Activities
for Mountain Lion Trailmen

Two may replace a missed Step or 'Hit the Trail!'
Activity at the Trail Guide's discretion. See the
complete guidelines at the beginning of this section.

☐ Discuss being a good friend to others with your parents. Think of a way each of you can do something good for another and commit to doing that.

☐ Read and review Matthew 6:14-15. Discuss a time when you have needed forgiveness or been forgiven. **CREATION 2b,c**

☐ Discuss the characteristics and qualities of good leaders. Think about characteristics members of your family have, and discuss ways to develop leadership skills and choose good role models.

☐ Discuss conservation and good stewardship with your family. **STEWARDSHIP 5a,b** Review home conservation practices.

☐ Discuss how to care for our country's flag. If you do not have your own flag at home, you may want to purchase one and hang it in a place of honor and respect.

☐ Discuss the fruits of the Spirit (Galatians 5:22-23) with your family. **HUMAN DIGNITY 3a,b** How can you develop and incorporate these qualities in your daily lives? Commit to demonstrate a behavior this week.

☐ As a family, do something for your neighbors: bake cookies as a gift, visit neighbors and ask them about their Christmas traditions or their favorite Christmas memories, sing Christmas carols, or help a neighbor with yard work.

☐ Fortitude is strength of mind that enables a person to encounter danger or bear pain or adversity with courage; synonyms include bravery and courage. Discuss fortitude. Challenge each other to

110 WOODLANDS TRAIL HANDBOOK

find scripture stories and other popular stories that show examples.

☐ Visit the "Focus on the Family" website to complete a personality profile on your child (*use the QR code below*). Have the family discuss their own personality types and how these types have helped them in their jobs and their lives. Also consider discussing how their personality types have influenced choices they have made.

family home activities

☐ Discuss different careers that focus on justice. Find a contact to learn more about his or her job or research online together.

☐ Discuss commitment and loyalty with your family. Talk about the loyalty cards that some stores offer to reward customers for repeat visits. Discuss any loyalty programs you are a part of and visit the store together. Discuss the rewards of commitment and loyalty in life.

☐ Visit a war memorial. Talk about what a memorial is and its importance. If possible, discover the history of the war commemorated by the memorial.

☐ Participate in a service project together.

Focus on the Family Personality Test, Standard

how do we track
advancements?

If your Trailman is beginning in the **Fox patrol,** begin tracking his advancements on page 113.

If your Trailman is beginning in the **Hawk patrol,** begin tracking his advancements on page 119.

If your Trailman is beginning in the **Mountain Lion patrol,** begin tracking his advancements on page 125.

Our robust advancement program for boys is both inspirational and fun. What a great opportunity to engage the whole family in this process. That can surely strengthen family bonds and help everyone grow spiritually! You can't measure it in a chart, but it's not any less real!

joining requirements

	DATE	TRAIL GUIDE INITIALS
I memorized the Oath COMPLETED ☐		
I learned the Sign COMPLETED ☐		
I learned the Salute COMPLETED ☐		
I learned the Handshake COMPLETED ☐		
I can recite the Pledge COMPLETED ☐		

You've earned your Fox Branch Patch!

Turn the page to start tracking your Bronze Branches for your Branch Patch!

Parents: Find the Woodlands Trailmap wall poster in our online store for your son to celebrate his achievements at home!

WOODLANDS TRAILMAP FOR FOXES

		Heritage Branch	Hobbies Branch	Life Skills Branch	
CORE Step	DATE STEP # TRAIL GUIDE INITIALS				
CORE Step	DATE STEP # TRAIL GUIDE INITIALS		This step not required for this Branch.		
CORE Step	DATE STEP # TRAIL GUIDE INITIALS	This step not required for this Branch.	This step not required for this Branch.		
ELECTIVE Step	DATE STEP # TRAIL GUIDE INITIALS				
ELECTIVE Step	DATE STEP # TRAIL GUIDE INITIALS	This step not required for this Branch.		This step not required for this Branch.	
Hit the Trail	DATE TRAIL GUIDE INITIALS				
BRONZE BRANCH PIN RECEIVED		COMPLETED ☐	COMPLETED ☐	COMPLETED ☐	

Well done, Trailman!

You've learned so much!
Congratulations!

Outdoor Skills *Branch*	Science & Technology *Branch*	Sports & Fitness *Branch*	Values *Branch*
	This step not required for this Branch.	This step not required for this Branch.	
This step not required for this Branch.	This step not required for this Branch.	This step not required for this Branch.	This step not required for this Branch.
COMPLETED ☐	COMPLETED ☐	COMPLETED ☐	COMPLETED ☐

Fox Branch Patch

COMPLETED! ☐

Turn the page to start tracking your bronze Sylvan Stars on your Forest Award!

FOREST AWARD

		Heritage *Branch*	Hobbies *Branch*	Life Skills *Branch*
CORE Step	DATE			
	STEP #			
	TRAIL GUIDE INITIALS			
CORE Step	DATE		This step not required for this Branch.	
	STEP #			
	TRAIL GUIDE INITIALS			
CORE Step	DATE	This step not required for this Branch.	This step not required for this Branch.	
	STEP #			
	TRAIL GUIDE INITIALS			
ELECTIVE Step	DATE			
	STEP #			
	TRAIL GUIDE INITIALS			
ELECTIVE Step	DATE	This step not required for this Branch.		This step not required for this Branch.
	STEP #			
	TRAIL GUIDE INITIALS			
Hit the Trail	DATE			
	TRAIL GUIDE INITIALS			
		COMPLETED ☐	COMPLETED ☐	COMPLETED ☐
BRONZE SYLVAN STAR RECEIVED		★	★	★

Way to go, Trailman!

Keep "Walking Worthy!"

116 WOODLANDS TRAIL HANDBOOK

Outdoor Skills *Branch*	Science & Technology *Branch*	Sports & Fitness *Branch*	Values *Branch*
	This step not required for this Branch.	This step not required for this Branch.	
This step not required for this Branch.	This step not required for this Branch.	This step not required for this Branch.	This step not required for this Branch.
COMPLETED ☐	COMPLETED ☐	COMPLETED ☐	COMPLETED ☐
★	★	★	★

You've earned all the Sylvan Stars for your Forest Award! ☐

FOREST AWARD

HOW DO WE TRACK ADVANCEMENTS? 117

worthy life award

	DATE	TRAIL GUIDE INITIALS
DEVOTIONAL ACTIVITY		
DISCIPLESHIP ACTIVITY		
DISCIPLINE ACTIVITIES (1)		
(2)		
(3)		
DEMONSTRATION ACTIVITY		

Worth Life Award

RECEIVED

Not everyone earns this award. It's a great goal.

You can earn a cross at each level!

118 WOODLANDS TRAIL HANDBOOK

joining requirements

	DATE	TRAIL GUIDE INITIALS
I memorized the Oath — COMPLETED ☐		
I learned the Sign — COMPLETED ☐		
I learned the Salute — COMPLETED ☐		
I learned the Handshake — COMPLETED ☐		
I memorized the Pledge — COMPLETED ☐		

You've earned your Hawk Branch Patch!

Turn the page to start tracking your Silver Branches for your Branch Patch!

Parents: Find the Woodlands Trailmap wall poster in our online store for your son to celebrate his achievements at home!

HOW DO WE TRACK ADVANCEMENTS?

		Heritage Branch	Hobbies Branch	Life Skills Branch	
CORE Step	DATE				
	STEP #				
	TRAIL GUIDE INITIALS				
CORE Step	DATE		This step not required for this Branch.		
	STEP #				
	TRAIL GUIDE INITIALS				
CORE Step	DATE	This step not required for this Branch.	This step not required for this Branch.		
	STEP #				
	TRAIL GUIDE INITIALS				
ELECTIVE Step	DATE				
	STEP #				
	TRAIL GUIDE INITIALS				
ELECTIVE Step	DATE	This step not required for this Branch.		This step not required for this Branch.	
	STEP #				
	TRAIL GUIDE INITIALS				
Hit the Trail	DATE				
	TRAIL GUIDE INITIALS				
		COMPLETED ☐	COMPLETED ☐	COMPLETED ☐	
	SILVER BRANCH PIN RECEIVED				

Well done, Trailman!

You've learned so much! Congratulations!

120 WOODLANDS TRAIL HANDBOOK

Outdoor Skills *Branch*	Science & Technology *Branch*	Sports & Fitness *Branch*	Values *Branch*
	This step not required for this Branch.	This step not required for this Branch.	
This step not required for this Branch.	This step not required for this Branch.	This step not required for this Branch.	This step not required for this Branch.
COMPLETED ☐	COMPLETED ☐	COMPLETED ☐	COMPLETED ☐

Hawk Branch Patch

COMPLETED! ☐

Turn the page to start tracking your silver Sylvan Stars on your Forest Award!

HOW DO WE TRACK ADVANCEMENTS?

FOREST AWARD

		Heritage *Branch*	Hobbies *Branch*	Life Skills *Branch*
CORE Step	DATE			
	STEP #			
	TRAIL GUIDE INITIALS			
CORE Step	DATE		This step not required for this Branch.	
	STEP #			
	TRAIL GUIDE INITIALS			
CORE Step	DATE	This step not required for this Branch.	This step not required for this Branch.	
	STEP #			
	TRAIL GUIDE INITIALS			
ELECTIVE Step	DATE			
	STEP #			
	TRAIL GUIDE INITIALS			
ELECTIVE Step	DATE	This step not required for this Branch.		This step not required for this Branch.
	STEP #			
	TRAIL GUIDE INITIALS			
Hit the Trail	DATE			
	TRAIL GUIDE INITIALS			
SILVER SYLVAN STAR RECEIVED		COMPLETED ☐	COMPLETED ☐	COMPLETED ☐

Wow!!

You are really making progress!

122 WOODLANDS TRAIL HANDBOOK

	Outdoor Skills *Branch*	Science & Technology *Branch*	Sports & Fitness *Branch*	Values *Branch*
....				
....				
....				
....				
....		This step not required for this Branch.	This step not required for this Branch.	
....				
....				
....				
....	This step not required for this Branch.	This step not required for this Branch.	This step not required for this Branch.	This step not required for this Branch.
....				
....				
	COMPLETED ☐	COMPLETED ☐	COMPLETED ☐	COMPLETED ☐

You've earned all the Sylvan Stars for your Forest Award! ☐

FOREST AWARD

HOW DO WE TRACK ADVANCEMENTS? 123

worthy life award

WORTHY LIFE
TRAIL LIFE USA

Worth Life Award

RECEIVED ☐

	DATE	TRAIL GUIDE INITIALS
DEVOTIONAL ACTIVITY	☐	☐
DISCIPLESHIP ACTIVITIES (1)	☐	☐
(2)	☐	☐
DISCIPLINE ACTIVITIES (1)	☐	☐
(2)	☐	☐
(3)	☐	☐
DEMONSTRATION ACTIVITY	☐	☐

The Worthy Life Award is one of my favorites!

joining requirements

	DATE	TRAIL GUIDE INITIALS
I memorized the Oath COMPLETED ☐		
I learned the Sign COMPLETED ☐		
I learned the Salute COMPLETED ☐		
I learned the Handshake COMPLETED ☐		
I memorized the Pledge COMPLETED ☐		
I properly folded the American Flag COMPLETED ☐		

You've earned your Mountain Lion Branch Patch!

Turn the page to start tracking your Gold Branches for your Branch Patch!

Parents:
Find the Woodlands Trailmap wall poster in our online store.

WOODLANDS TRAILMAP FOR MOUNTAIN

HOW DO WE TR

		Heritage *Branch*	Hobbies *Branch*	Life Skills *Branch*
CORE Step	DATE			
	STEP #			
	TRAIL GUIDE INITIALS			
CORE Step	DATE		This step not required for this Branch.	
	STEP #			
	TRAIL GUIDE INITIALS			
CORE Step	DATE	This step not required for this Branch.	This step not required for this Branch.	
	STEP #			
	TRAIL GUIDE INITIALS			
ELECTIVE Step	DATE			
	STEP #			
	TRAIL GUIDE INITIALS			
ELECTIVE Step	DATE	This step not required for this Branch.		This step not required for this Branch.
	STEP #			
	TRAIL GUIDE INITIALS			
Hit the Trail	DATE			
	TRAIL GUIDE INITIALS			
	COMPLETED	☐	☐	☐
	GOLD BRANCH PIN RECEIVED			

Well done, Trailman!

You've learned so much! Congratulations!

Outdoor Skills *Branch*	Science & Technology *Branch*	Sports & Fitness *Branch*	Values *Branch*
	This step not required for this Branch.	This step not required for this Branch.	
This step not required for this Branch.	This step not required for this Branch.	This step not required for this Branch.	This step not required for this Branch.
COMPLETED ☐	COMPLETED ☐	COMPLETED ☐	COMPLETED ☐

Mountain Lion Branch Patch

COMPLETED!
☐

Turn the page to start tracking your gold Sylvan Stars on your Forest Award!

FOREST AWARD

		Heritage *Branch*	Hobbies *Branch*	Life Skills *Branch*
CORE Step	DATE			
	STEP #			
	TRAIL GUIDE INITIALS			
CORE Step	DATE		This step not required for this Branch.	
	STEP #			
	TRAIL GUIDE INITIALS			
CORE Step	DATE	This step not required for this Branch.	This step not required for this Branch.	
	STEP #			
	TRAIL GUIDE INITIALS			
ELECTIVE Step	DATE			
	STEP #			
	TRAIL GUIDE INITIALS			
ELECTIVE Step	DATE	This step not required for this Branch.		This step not required for this Branch.
	STEP #			
	TRAIL GUIDE INITIALS			
Hit the Trail	DATE			
	TRAIL GUIDE INITIALS			
		COMPLETED ☐	COMPLETED ☐	COMPLETED ☐
	GOLD SYLVAN STAR RECEIVED	★	★	★

That's what I call "Walking Worthy!"

128 WOODLANDS TRAIL HANDBOOK

Outdoor Skills Branch	Science & Technology Branch	Sports & Fitness Branch	Values Branch
	This step not required for this Branch.	This step not required for this Branch.	
This step not required for this Branch.	This step not required for this Branch.	This step not required for this Branch.	This step not required for this Branch.
COMPLETED ☐	COMPLETED ☐	COMPLETED ☐	COMPLETED ☐

You've earned all the Sylvan Stars for your Forest Award! ☐

FOREST AWARD

HOW DO WE TRACK ADVANCEMENTS? 129

worthy life award

	DATE	TRAIL GUIDE INITIALS
DEVOTIONAL ACTIVITY		
DISCIPLESHIP ACTIVITIES (1)		
(2)		
DISCIPLINE ACTIVITIES (1)		
(2)		
(3)		
DEMONSTRATION ACTIVITY		

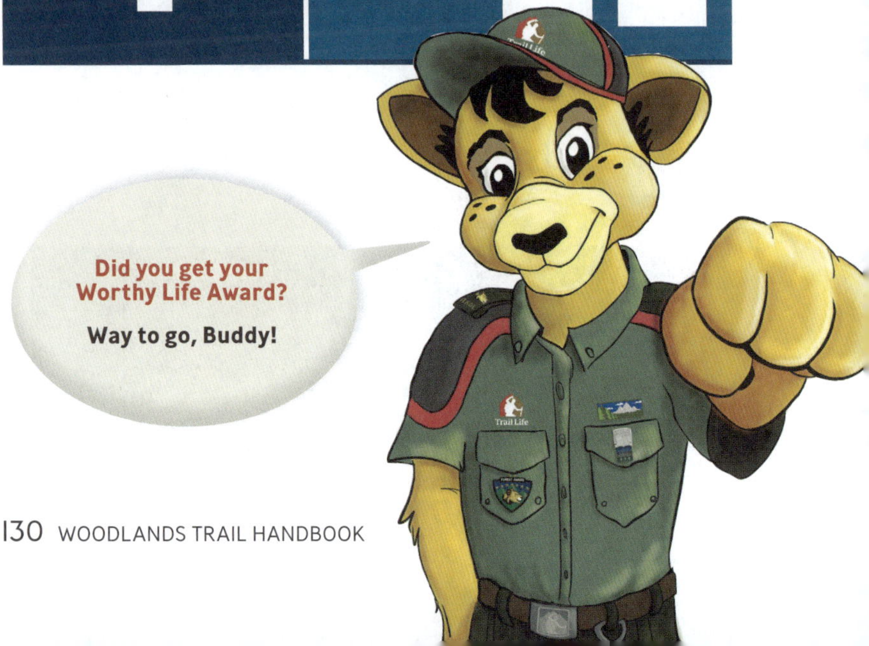

WORTHY LIFE
TRAIL LIFE USA

Worth Life Award

RECEIVED ☐

Did you get your Worthy Life Award?

Way to go, Buddy!

130 WOODLANDS TRAIL HANDBOOK

fireguard award

	DATE	TRAIL GUIDE INITIALS
APPROPRIATE FIRES		
SAFETY CIRCLE		
DANGERS		
TREAD LIGHTLY!®		
SAFETY TOOLS FOR CAMPFIRES		
CAMPFIRE PIT		
TYPES OF FUEL		
LIGHTING SAFETY		
BUILD A FIRE		
UNATTENDED FIRES		
WHAT TO KEEP OUT OF A FIRE		
EXTINGUISH A FIRE		

COMPLETED ☐

FIREGUARD

FIREGUARD

Trailman's Name

Troop # _____

Adult Troop Leader

HOW DO WE TRACK ADVANCEMENTS? 131

woodsman award

	DATE	TRAIL GUIDE INITIALS
KNIFE IS A TOOL		
APPROPRIATE TO CARRY		
SAFETY CIRCLE		
PASSING AND RECEIVING		
OPENING AND CLOSING		
CUTTING SAFETY		
DANGEROUS KNIFE		
SHARPENING		
OILING		
CLEANING AND DRYING		
STORAGE		

COMPLETED

WOODSMAN

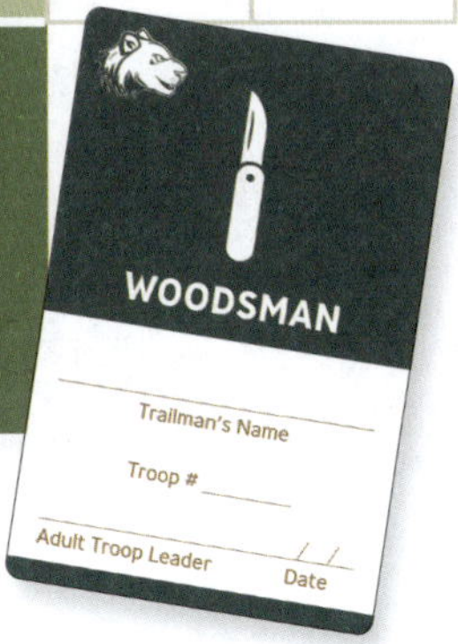

WOODSMAN

Trailman's Name

Troop #

Adult Troop Leader   Date

132 WOODLANDS TRAIL HANDBOOK

timberline award

	DATE	TRAIL GUIDE INITIALS
MOUNTAIN LION FOREST AWARD		
7 MOUNTAIN LION SYLVAN STARS		
INVITE A FRIEND		
ATTEND OVERNIGHT CAMPOUT		
RESPONSIBILITY		
SERVICE PROJECT		
MOUNTAIN LION WORTHY LIFE AWARD		

COMPLETED ☐

You've earned your Timberline Patch!

Congratulations! You've earned the highest award in the Woodlands Trail program!

Well done, Trailman!
This is a HUGE accomplishment!